# Lab Manual for MCDST Guide to

# Supporting Users and Troubleshooting Desktop Applications on a Microsoft® Windows® XP Operating System

## Jill Batistick

THOMSON

COURSE TECHNOLOGY

Australia • Canada • Mexico • Singapore • Spain • United Kingdom • United States

**THOMSON**

**COURSE TECHNOLOGY** ™

**Lab Manual for MCDST Guide to Supporting Users
and Troubleshooting Desktop Applications on a
Microsoft® Windows® XP Operating System**

by Jill Batistick

**Managing Editor:**
Will Pitkin III

**Senior Marketing Manager:**
Karen Seitz

**Copy Editor:**
Harry Johnson

**Product Manager:**
Manya Chylinski

**Senior Manufacturing Coordinator:**
Trevor Kallop

**Proofreader:**
Vicki Zimmer

**Developmental Editor:**
Lisa M. Lord

**Technical Edit/Quality Assurance:**
Chris Carvalho
John Freitas
Christian Kunciw
Burt LaFountain
Serge Palladino
Chris Scriver
Danielle Shaw
Marianne Snow

**Text Designer:**
GEX Publishing Services

**Production Editor:**
BobbiJo Frasca

**Compositor:**
GEX Publishing Services

**Associate Product Manager:**
Sarah Santoro

**Cover Design:**
Steve Deschene

**Editorial Assistant:**
Jennifer Smith

# TABLE OF CONTENTS

# INTRODUCTION

The objective of this lab manual is to assist you in preparing for the Microsoft Certification Exam 70-272: Supporting Users and Troubleshooting Desktop Applications on a Microsoft Windows XP Operating System by applying the objectives to relevant lab activities. This text is designed to be used with *MCDST Guide to Supporting Users and Troubleshooting Desktop Applications on a Microsoft Windows XP Operating System* (0-619-21602-6). Although this manual is written to be used in a classroom lab environment, it can also be used for self-study on a home network.

This manual provides the information you need to become proficient in the tasks expected of a desktop support technician (DST). Each chapter presents a series of labs with different goals that explore the nuances and intricacies of the operating system and related applications. Your instructor will supply answers to the review questions and additional information about the activities.

Microsoft released the latest service pack for Windows XP, Service Pack 2 (SP2), during the development of this book. In this book, the discussions, activities, and screen shots all reflect the appearance and functionality of the applications and Windows XP before SP2. Rewritten versions of activities and projects affected by the SP2 upgrade can be found on *www.course.com*.

## FEATURES

To ensure a successful experience for instructors and students alike, this book includes the following features:

- **Lab Objectives**—The goal of each lab is clearly stated at the beginning.
- **Materials Required**—Every lab includes information on hardware, software, and other materials you need to complete the lab.
- **Estimated Completion Time**—Every lab has an estimated completion time so that you can plan your activities more accurately.
- **Activity Background**—Activity Background information supplies important details and prepares students for the activity that follows.
- **Activity Sections**—Labs are presented in manageable sections and include figures to reinforce learning.
- **Step-by-Step Instructions**—Steps provide practice, which enhances technical proficiency.

- **Supporting Users and Troubleshooting Desktop Applications on a Microsoft Windows XP Operating System Certification Objectives**—For each chapter, the relevant objectives from Exam # 70–272 are listed.
- **Review Questions**—Review questions reinforce the concepts presented in labs.

## HARDWARE REQUIREMENTS

The following minimum hardware is needed to perform the labs in this manual:

- Pentium 233 MHz (550 MHz or higher is recommended)
- 128 MB RAM (256 MB RAM is recommended)
- 2 GB of free space after installing Windows XP and Office 2003 (4 GB of free space is recommended)
- CD-ROM and floppy disk drives

## SOFTWARE REQUIREMENTS

The following software is needed for the correct lab setup:

- Windows XP Professional with Service Pack 1a; use the default installation
- Microsoft Office 2003
- Norton AntiVirus
- One optional application that can be safely deleted
- Internet access

## ACKNOWLEDGEMENTS

I would like to thank the following reviewers, whose insightful comments have proved invaluable in developing this manual: David Courtaway, DeVry University, Pomona; Russ Davis, Pittsburgh Technical Institute; Rachelle Hall, Glendale Community College, Arizona; and Peggy Mooney, College of Alameda.

Many thanks go to Lisa Lord, Editor Extraordinaire, and Manya Chylinski, Supreme PM, for their guidance on this project. A team like ours doesn't come around very often.

Of course, final thanks goes to the large scorpion who recently fell from the ceiling fan onto my mouse pad; your appearance brightened an otherwise dull day.

# INTRODUCTION TO SUPPORTING USERS

**Labs included in this chapter:**

➤ Lab 1.1 Understanding the Desktop Support Technician's Responsibilities
➤ Lab 1.2 Viewing System Information
➤ Lab 1.3 Creating a Local User Account
➤ Lab 1.4 Using Network Diagnostics

Although the labs in this chapter pertain to knowledge and skills desktop support technicians should have to fulfill their job responsibilities, they don't map directly to any MCDST certification objectives.

---

# Lab 1.1 Understanding the Desktop Support Technician's Responsibilities

## Objectives

The goal of this lab is to understand the desktop support technician's (DST's) role in supporting users. Note that the role varies from company to company; your job is to adapt to each company's environment.

## Materials Required

This lab requires the following:

➤ Paper and pencil

Estimated completion time: 30 minutes

## Activity Background

Although the terminology, position titles, and even responsibilities vary slightly, depending on a company's organizational structure, the basic concepts of a desktop support technician's (DST's) role remain the same.

Some of the generic terms used in this manual include the following:

➤ *Call*—A contact with the first line of support. It might be a phone call to the help desk, an e-mail to the support department, an in-person discussion with the help desk or support personnel, or a Web-based intranet report form.

➤ *Incident*—The issue being reported.

➤ *Problem*—The cause of the incident.

➤ *Solution*—The method used to return the system to a normal operating state or to eliminate the problem.

In a large organization, a help desk is often the first contact for users to get help. In some organizations, the help desk is staffed with DSTs who can usually solve the majority of user problems quickly. Other organizations staff help desks with entry-level personnel or even temporary contract workers, who might have minimal DST skills. These personnel are responsible for recording information about users' problems in an incident-tracking software program, such as Track-IT or Robo-Help. Sometimes they have other basic responsibilities, such as resetting passwords and looking in a locally maintained database (called a *knowledge base*) for simple fixes to common problems. User problems are then assigned to a DST if more complex skills are needed to help users.

Regardless of the structure, whether DSTs are the first-level or second-level contact, they need to have the skills to ascertain quickly whether an incident is within their realm of responsibility and knowledge or a higher-level support technician needs to become involved. Moving an incident to a higher-level technician is referred to as *escalation*.

In the following scenarios, you determine whether the tasks are the responsibility of a DST. Note that there's no one right answer; in addition, your answer in the real world would depend on your company's internal organization and culture.

**LAB ACTIVITY**

## ACTIVITY

**Scenario 1:** "I got to work this morning and tried to log on to my computer. I tried about a dozen times and finally called you. Why can't I log on? I have never had this problem before."

Does this problem fall into an average DST's responsibilities? Record your answer here. Explain why or why not and list some potential solutions you might recommend.

_____

_____

_____

_____

_____

_____

**Scenario 2:** "I have been working all morning on a report that is due. When I send it to the printer, it doesn't print, but I don't get any error messages on my screen. I have walked down to the printer several times and still nothing. The others around me are getting their documents to print. I need that report for a meeting in 20 minutes. Please help me."

Does this problem fall into an average DST's responsibilities? Record your answer here. Explain why or why not and list some potential solutions you might recommend.

_____

_____

_____

_____

_____

**Scenario 3:** "Something is wrong with my computer. It keeps shutting down, and I have to restart it about every five minutes. It worked fine when I left work yesterday. All I have been able to do so far this morning is check my e-mail, but I haven't even finished that yet because this &@!^$#$&* computer won't keep running long enough for me to read the rest of my e-mail. I think this computer has a bad power supply that needs to get changed. Can you come and change it right away?"

Does this problem fall into an average DST's responsibilities? Record your answer here. Explain why or why not and list some potential solutions you might recommend.

_____

_____

_____

_____

_____

_____

**Scenario 4:** "I am trying to create a sales report with all the sales figures for the past three months. I know there's a way to make this spreadsheet automatically calculate all the columns, but I can't figure out how. I want to be able to use this spreadsheet as a template for our weekly sales meeting. I just want to change the daily sales amount for the new week and have the spreadsheet calculate the new sales numbers correctly. Do you know how I can make it do that?"

Does this problem fall into an average DST's responsibilities? Record your answer here. Explain why or why not and list some potential solutions you might recommend.

_____

_____

_____

_____

_____

_____

**Scenario 5:** "I just bought a new Sony DVD for creating marketing presentations to send out to customers about our new prototypes. I need to learn how to do video editing so that I can create a nice-looking presentation. Will you come and install the DVD drive and the software on my computer, and then teach me how to edit stills and motion video for the presentation? It comes with video-editing software, so we don't even have to buy anything else."

Does this problem fall into an average DST's responsibilities? Record your answer here. Explain why or why not and list some potential solutions you might recommend.

_____

_____

_____

_____

_____

_____

## Certification Objectives

Objectives for Microsoft Exam #70-272: Supporting Users and Troubleshooting Desktop Applications on a Microsoft Windows XP Operating System:

➤ None—Informational only

## Review Questions

1. In an organization's support department, a knowledge base consists of which of the following?

    a. a collection of system resources

    b. a collection of calls, incidents, problems, and solutions

    c. a collection of vendor product specifications

    d. a collection of configuration records

2. When a help desk support person or a DST is unable to solve a problem, the problem is sent to the next higher level, a process called _____ .

    a. encapsulation

    b. up-tiering

    c. escalation

    d. downplaying

3. Typical DST responsibilities include which of the following? (Choose all that apply.)

    a. configuring Internet settings

    b. identifying network connection problems

    c. installing Microsoft Office 2003

    d. configuring Layer 3 switches

4. Typical DSTs need to include which of the following skills in their personal toolkits? (Choose all that apply.)

   a. software installation skills

   b. operating system configuration skills

   c. customer service skills

   d. software knowledge

5. DSTs regularly use which of the following tools to perform their responsibilities? (Choose all that apply.)

   a. the organization's knowledge base

   b. the Microsoft Knowledge Base

   c. application vendors' knowledge bases

   d. hardware and software vendor resource kits

## Lab 1.2 Viewing System Information

### Objectives

The goal of this lab is to learn that often several methods are available for reviewing and gathering system or network information.

### Materials Required

This lab requires the following:

➤ A computer running Microsoft Windows XP

➤ Administrative rights on the computer

Estimated completion time: 20 minutes

### Activity Background

A DST must be versatile and flexible and know how to find different solutions to problems. As with all Microsoft products, there are usually several ways to perform the same task. Sometimes, it's simply a matter of preference. For example, you can save a file by choosing File, Save from the menu bar, by clicking the Save icon on the toolbar, or by using the keyboard shortcut Ctrl+S. All three methods accomplish the same goal.

Likewise, many tools are available to technicians to support the operating system (OS) or applications. Several tools have graphic user interfaces (GUIs) you can use to gather information, and often there are corresponding command-line tools. Although deciding which tool to use can be just a matter of preference, sometimes a tool or utility is available only in GUI or command-line format. A DST needs to be knowledgeable about all the utilities and formats available. At times, the GUI won't be available because of a corrupted file or maybe because you're unable start the operating system. Knowing how to use the correct tools in a command-line environment is an invaluable skill for DSTs.

**LAB ACTIVITY**

## ACTIVITY

1. Log on to a computer. You need to be able to log on with administrative rights.

2. Click **Start**, **Help and Support**. Under the Pick a task section, click **Use Tools to view your computer information and diagnose problems**, as shown in Figure 1-1.

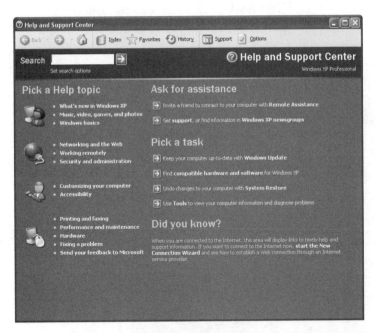

**Figure 1-1**    Options available in the Help and Support Center

3. In the Tools pane on the left, click **My Computer Information**.

4. In the right pane, click **View general system information about this computer** to open a window showing information about your computer in several different panes: Specifications, Operating System, Memory (RAM), Processor, General Computer Info, and Local Disk. *Do not close this window.*

5. Close all other open windows.

6. Click **Start**, **Run**, and type **cmd**, as shown in Figure 1-2. Press **Enter** (or click **OK**).

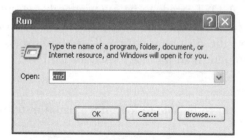

**Figure 1-2**    Opening a command-prompt window

7. You are now accessing a command-prompt window, sometimes referred to as a DOS prompt. Type **SYSTEMINFO**, and then press **Enter**.

8. Review the results, which will look similar to Figure 1-3.

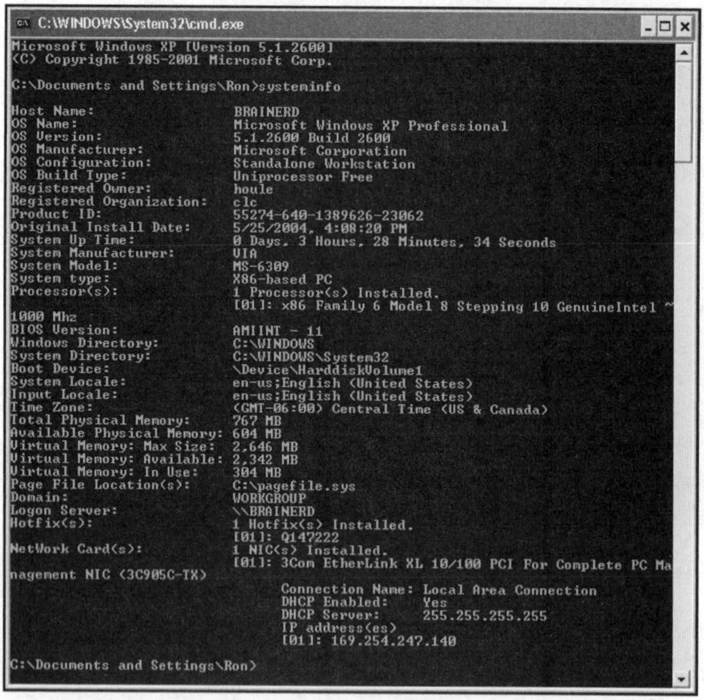

**Figure 1-3**    Command-line System Information results

9. Compare the information you retrieved with the SYSTEMINFO command to the information you saw in the Help and Support GUI window. Record the similarities and differences.

10. Close all open windows.

11. Repeat Steps 2 and 3.

12. In the right pane, click **View a list of Microsoft software installed on this computer**. Review the components of the window. *Do not close this window.*

13. Close all other open windows.

14. Click **Start**, **Control Panel**. If necessary, click **Switch to Classic View**. You see the applets you can open to configure different OS components.

15. Double-click the **Add or Remove Programs** icon to see a list of currently installed programs. The window should look similar to Figure 1-4, although your list of installed programs will likely vary.

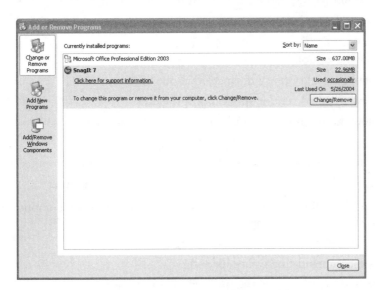

**Figure 1-4**   The Add or Remove Programs window

16. Compare the information you retrieved with this Control Panel applet to the information you saw in the Help and Support GUI window. Record the similarities and differences.

17. Close all open windows, and log off.

## Certification Objectives

Objectives for Microsoft Exam #70-272: Supporting Users and Troubleshooting Desktop Applications on a Microsoft Windows XP Operating System:

➤  None—Informational only

## Review Questions

1. Which of the following options are available when you're searching for tools in the My Computer Information category in Help and Support? (Choose all that apply.)

   a. View general system information about this computer

   b. View installed vendor application programs

   c. View the status of my system hardware and software

   d. View the status of network configurations

   e. Find information about the hardware installed on this computer

   f. View a list of Microsoft software installed on this computer

2. You can find the amount of RAM installed in a computer by using which of the following options? (Choose all that apply.)

   a. View general system information about this computer

   b. View installed vendor application programs

   c. View the status of my system hardware and software

   d. View the status of network configurations

   e. Find information about the hardware installed on this computer

   f. View a list of Microsoft software installed on this computer

3. Which of the following options or tools enables you to see a computer's IP address? (Choose all that apply.)

   a. View general system information about this computer

   b. The command-line utility Ipconfig

   c. View the status of my system hardware and software

   d. View the status of network configurations

   e. Find information about the hardware installed on this computer

   f. View a list of Microsoft software installed on this computer

4. You can find the Add or Remove Programs applet in _____ .

   a. View general system information about this computer

   b. View the status of my system hardware and software

     c. Find information about the hardware installed on this computer

     d. Control Panel

5. The Control Panel is the preferred location for making changes to the system configuration that result in changes to the Registry database. True or False?

## LAB 1.3 CREATING A LOCAL USER ACCOUNT

### Objectives

The goal of this lab is to learn how to use the Microsoft Management Console (MMC) framework and to design custom desktop tool sets for administering and troubleshooting common OS components.

### Materials Required

This lab requires the following:

➤ A computer running Microsoft Windows XP

➤ Administrative rights on the computer

Estimated completion time: 30 minutes

### Activity Background

Microsoft has extensive resources available to support technicians. In Lab 1-2, you tried several methods of getting information from the Help and Support Center and with command-line utilities. Another invaluable tool for DSTs is the MMC, which is simply a framework for adding tools and utilities according to your needs. In other words, it's a customizable window (framework) where you can add administrative tools that best meet your needs. In the following activity, you use this console to add a user to your system.

LAB ACTIVITY

### ACTIVITY

1. Log on to a computer. You need to be able to log on with administrative rights.

2. Click **Start**, right-click **My Computer**, and click **Manage** to open the Computer Management MMC.

3. Many tools are available in this MMC. The three broad categories of System Tools, Storage, and Services and Applications have many subcategories of tools grouped by the tool's general function and the OS component it's intended to address. To use this tool to add users to a system, first click to expand **System Tools** (if necessary), click to expand **Local Users and Groups** (if necessary), and click **Users**.

4. In the right pane, view the users currently listed on your system. (Your screen should resemble Figure 1-5.)

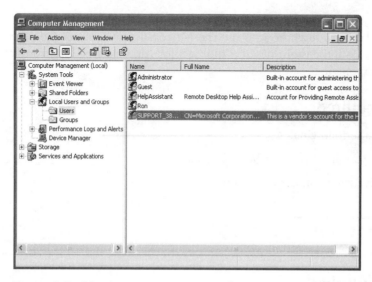

**Figure 1-5** Viewing user accounts in the Computer Management MMC

5. Now add a new user named Zachary Brady with a password of P@55w0rd and a user name of zbrady*xx* (*xx* is your student number). One way to do this is to click **Action**, **New User** from the menu. Click **Close** so that you can try the second method in Step 6.

6. Right-click a blank area in the right pane, and click **New User**.

7. In the New User dialog box, type in the information shown in Figure 1-6, but add the student number your instructor assigned to the end of the user name. Click to clear the **User must change password at next logon** check box, and click to select the **Account is disabled** check box.

8. Click the **Create** button, and then click **Close**. Review your users in the right pane to see the new user you just created. Notice the red X next to the account name, meaning the account is disabled. When an account is disabled, no one can log on to the system using that account.

1

New User                                    [?][X]

User name:     zbrady

Full name:     Zachary Brady

Description:   Sales Employee starting January 15, 2005

Password:      ••••••••

Confirm password:   ••••••••

☐ User must change password at next logon
☐ User cannot change password
☐ Password never expires
☑ Account is disabled

                    [  Create  ]   [  Close  ]

**Figure 1-6**   Adding information in the New User dialog box

9. Double-click the **zbradyxx** account to open the Properties dialog box for this user. Click to clear the **Account is disabled** check box. Click to select the **Password never expires** check box (see Figure 1-7), and then click **OK**. Notice that the red X next to the account name is gone because the account is now enabled. Also notice that you haven't yet seen an option for changing the user's password.

10. To change the user's password, right-click the **zbradyxx** user account, and click **Set Password**.

11. In the warning message box, read the warning and click **Help**. Resetting passwords in this manner causes users to lose access to encrypted files stored with EFS, encrypted e-mail, and some Internet stored passwords. Click **Cancel** and close the help window.

**NOTE**

You might have no choice and be required to change users' passwords with the method in Step 10 if they have forgotten their passwords. In a domain environment, you can reset a domain password without losing access to the user's encrypted files or use the Recovery Agent to retrieve encrypted files for users.

12. In the Computer Management window, collapse **System Tools**, expand **Services and Applications**, click **Services**, and then scroll to and double-click **Workstation** in the right pane.

**Figure 1-7**   Selecting password options in the Properties dialog box

13. In the Workstation Properties dialog box, click the **Dependencies** tab. Notice how many OS components depend on this service running properly. Close the dialog box, and then close the Computer Management MMC.

14. To build a custom MMC, click **Start**, **Run**, type **mmc**, and press **Enter**. You should have an empty customizable MMC framework.

15. Click **File**, **Add/Remove Snap-in** from the menu.

16. In the Add/Remove Snap-in dialog box, click **Add**. Review the available standalone snap-ins you could load. Notice that Computer Management is one of the available snap-ins. Selecting this option would create the same MMC you used in the previous steps. In the Add Standalone Snap-in dialog box, click **Local Users and Groups**, and then click **Add**.

17. Verify that the Local computer option is selected in the Choose Target Machine dialog box. Click **Finish**.

18. In the Add Standalone Snap-in dialog box, click **Event Viewer** in the list of snap-ins, and then click **Add**. Click **Finish**, and then click **Close** in the Add Standalone Snap-in dialog box.

19. Click **OK** in the Add/Remove Snap-in dialog box. You have now created a custom MMC with the Local Users and Groups tool and the Event Viewer tool. To save this custom MMC to your desktop, click **File**, **Save** from the menu, and in the Save in list box, click **Desktop**. In the File name text box, type **My MMC**, and then click **Save**.

20. Close all open windows.

21. On the desktop, double-click **My MMC**. Review the tools you loaded for your custom MMC. Find the user account zbrady*xx*.

22. Close all windows, and log off.

## Certification Objectives

Objectives for Microsoft Exam #70-272: Supporting Users and Troubleshooting Desktop Applications on a Microsoft Windows XP Operating System:

➤ None—Informational only

## Review Questions

1. *MMC* stands for _____ .
   a. Microsoft Media Configuration
   b. Microsoft Manage and Configure
   c. Microsoft Management Configuration
   d. Microsoft Management Console

2. To customize the MMC's look and functionality, you can add which of the following?
   a. utilities
   b. snap consoles
   c. snap-ins
   d. command lines

3. Which component would you add to the MMC so that you could add users?
   a. Event Viewer
   b. Local Policy
   c. Disk Defragment
   d. Local Users and Groups

4. Which of the following is not an available snap-in?
   a. Network Monitor
   b. Certificates

      c. Shared Folders

      d. Group Policy

5. Explain why the MMC is a valuable tool for DSTs.

_____

_____

_____

_____

_____

# LAB 1.4 USING NETWORK DIAGNOSTICS

## Objectives

The goal of this lab is to learn how to use Network Diagnostics on your system. Learning to use this tool helps you produce information about a system that can be sent to other team members. In addition, if you need information from an end user, you can ask him or her to run this tool and send you the resulting file via e-mail.

## Materials Required

This lab requires the following:

➤ A computer running Microsoft Windows XP

➤ Administrative rights on the computer

Estimated completion time: 15 minutes

## Activity Background

Network Diagnostics is one of the many tools you can access via Help and Support on your computer. You can gather basic information, such as the operating system version and modem information, or you can gather detailed information, such as the availability of the Mail and News services. Regardless of the detail level you need, this tool will prove useful.

**LAB ACTIVITY**

## ACTIVITY

1. Click **Start**, **Help and Support**, and then click **Use Tools to view your computer information and diagnose problems**.

2. Click **Network Diagnostics** in the Tools list box, and then click **Set scanning options** in the pane on the right. Your screen should resemble Figure 1-8.

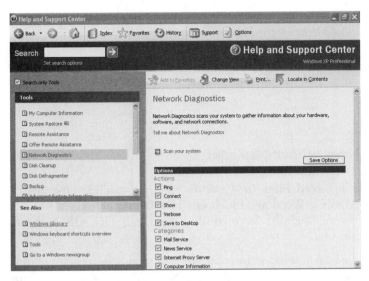

**Figure 1-8**   Options in Network Diagnostics

3. In the Actions list on the right, click the **Verbose** check box, and then click the **Save to Desktop** check box, if necessary. Click to clear the **Ping** and **Connect** check boxes.

4. In the Categories list, click to clear the following check boxes: **Mail Service**, **News Service**, and **Internet Proxy Server**.

5. Click the **Save Options** button, and then click the **Scan your system** link. After a few moments, your screen should resemble Figure 1-9.

6. If your system shows any FAILED categories, expand those categories and read the related information.

7. Under Computer Information, click to expand **Operating System** and view the resulting information.

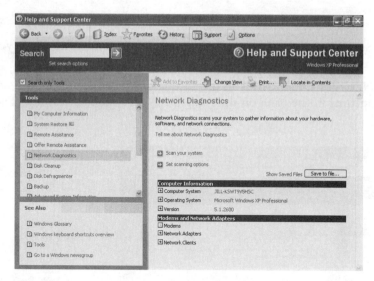

**Figure 1-9**    Results from Network Diagnostics

8. Click **Show Saved Files**. In Windows Explorer, you'll see the files that have been saved to C:\Windows\PCHealth\HelpCtr\System\NetDiag. Close Windows Explorer. Click the **Save to file** button, and click **OK** in the resulting information box.

9. Minimize all open windows so that you can view your desktop. Find and open the resulting .htm file on your desktop. Note that you can expand and collapse options in this file by clicking plus and minus signs on the left side of the screen.

10. Close the .htm file. Close Help and Support.

## Certification Objectives

Objectives for Microsoft Exam #70-272: Supporting Users and Troubleshooting Desktop Applications on a Microsoft Windows XP Operating System:

➤  None—Informational only

## Review Questions

1. Which of the following is not a tool that's accessible via the Help and Support Center?

   a. My Computer Information

   b. Backup

   c. Disk Cleanup

   d. Block Remote Assistance

2. If you use Network Diagnostics to gather information about your system, which of the following is found under the Computer Information category of results?

    a. Default Outlook Express Mail

    b. Version

    c. Modems

    d. Network Clients

3. Under which of the following categories of Network Diagnostics output would you find information about network clients?

    a. Modems and Network Adapters

    b. Computer Information

    c. Internet Service

    d. none of the above

4. Your system must be connected to the Internet for you to run Network Diagnostics. True or False?

5. Which of the following paths leads you to output files from Network Diagnostics?

    a. C:\Windows\PCHealth\HelpCtr\System\NetDiag

    b. C:\System\NetDiag\Control Panel

    c. C:\Windows\System\NetDiag

    d. C:\Windows\My Computer\System\NetDiag

# OVERVIEW OF MICROSOFT USER APPLICATIONS

## Labs included in this chapter:

➤ Lab 2.1 Installing Office 2003 and Removing Office 2003 Components
➤ Lab 2.2 Troubleshooting Office 2003 Installation Problems
➤ Lab 2.3 Understanding Office Application Default Settings
➤ Lab 2.4 Reviewing Windows Applications

| Microsoft MCDST Exam #70-272 Objectives | |
|---|---|
| Objective | Lab |
| Configure and troubleshoot Office applications. | 2.1 |
| Answer end-user questions related to configuring Office applications. | 2.1 |
| Troubleshoot application installation problems. | 2.1, 2.2 |
| Answer end-user questions related to configuring the operating system to support an application. | 2.1, 2.2, 2 |
| Resolve issues related to Office application support features. Tasks include configuring Office applications and interpreting error messages. | 2.1, 2.3 |
| Answer end-user questions related to customizing Office applications. | 2.3 |
| Troubleshoot access to local resources. | 2.3 |
| Answer end-user questions related to customizing the operating system to support an application. | 2.3 |
| Configure and troubleshoot Internet Explorer. | 2.4 |

## LAB 2.1 INSTALLING OFFICE 2003 AND REMOVING OFFICE 2003 COMPONENTS

### Objectives

The goal of this lab is to successfully install Microsoft Office 2003 and then remove components of Office 2003. Desktop support technicians (DSTs) can expect to be involved with a variety of application installations.

### Materials Required

This lab requires the following:

➤ A computer running Windows XP with Service Pack 1a

➤ Administrative rights on the computer

➤ Microsoft Office 2003 Installation CD

Estimated completion time: 45 minutes

### Activity Background

DSTs are frequently called on to install application programs or troubleshoot their installations. The most popular desktop suite of programs includes the Microsoft Office Suite. DSTs must know and understand the installation process because they are usually the support mechanism for troubleshooting installations.

LAB ACTIVITY

### ACTIVITY

1. Log on to a computer. You need to be able to log on with administrative rights.

2. Insert the Microsoft Office 2003 installation CD. Press the **Caps Lock** key. In the subsequent window, type in your product key. Click **Next**.

3. Press the **Caps Lock** key again to toggle off this feature.

4. Type your name in the User name text box (if necessary), and type your initials in the Initials text box. (You can also type in an organization name, although this information isn't required.) Click **Next**.

5. Click the **I accept the terms in the License Agreement** check box in the End-User License Agreement window, and then click **Next**.

6. Click the **Complete Install** option button in the Type of Installation setup window, as shown in Figure 2-1. Note the default folder where the Office 2003 files will be copied. Click **Next**.

2

**NOTE** If you want to change this default installation folder, click the Browse button and select a different folder. If a user installed to a different installation folder, for example, you would need to identify which folder was used to effectively troubleshoot installation problems or Registry settings.

**Figure 2-1**  Choosing an installation type

7. In the Summary window, notice the Office 2003 applications that will be installed. This window also lists the disk space needed to install the components and how much disk space is available. For the installation used to write this lab, 934 MB of disk space is required, which includes space allocated and used by temporary files during the installation process. You can delete these temporary installation files later; they take up about 350 MB of the total required space. A complete installation takes about 580 MB of total disk space after the temporary installation files are deleted. Click **Install**.

8. Watch the install process on the monitor. Click **Finish**.

**NOTE** Clicking the Delete installation files check box, if available, removes the temporary installation log files. These files are useful for troubleshooting an installation. On the other hand, deleting these files would free up nearly 300 MB of disk space. Your choice in this matter depends on your objectives—more troubleshooting flexibility or more disk space.

9. Now that you have installed Microsoft Office 2003 successfully, you'll test an application from the suite and then uninstall one component. Click **Start**, point to **All Programs**, point to **Microsoft Office**, and click **Microsoft Office PowerPoint 2003**, as shown in Figure 2-2. (Click **Cancel** if the Activation window opens.) Notice that menu items for recently installed programs are displayed with a different colored background on your screen.

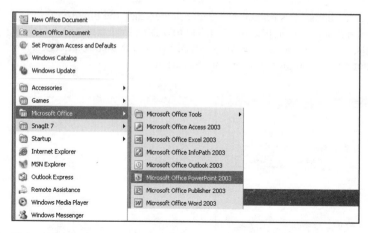

**Figure 2-2**   Opening PowerPoint

10. In PowerPoint, click the text **Click to add title**, and type your name. Click the text **Click to add subtitle**, and type **My Student Project**. Click **File**, **Save** from the menu, ensure that **My Documents** is the folder selected in the Save in list box, name the file **My test of PowerPoint**, and click **Save**. Close PowerPoint.

11. Click **Start**, **My Documents**, and then double-click **My test of PowerPoint** to open the PowerPoint file you created and saved. If the Activation window opens, click **Cancel**. The operating system is identifying your file as a Microsoft PowerPoint Presentation file. This is done through an operating system process and an application Registry setting called File Associations.

12. View your PowerPoint file and then close PowerPoint. With the My Documents folder still open, click **Tools**, **Folder Options** from the menu.

13. Click the **File Types** tab, and scroll down in the Registered file types list box until you see PPT under the Extensions column. Click **PPT**. In the Details section, notice that PPT files are opened with Microsoft Office PowerPoint. Make a mental note of this Details section because users frequently go into this File Types tab and change the program associated with a file extension, which stops the previously assigned program from starting when a user double-clicks a file. You need to reset the file association in this dialog box (or make a change in the Registry, which isn't recommended) to get the correct program to open when a user double-clicks a file.

14. Close all open windows.

15. To uninstall Microsoft Office or one or more of its components, you use the Add or Remove Programs applet in Control Panel. Click **Start**, **Control Panel**, **Add or Remove Programs**. Click the **Microsoft Office (Professional Edition) 2003** item (your edition might vary) to highlight it, if necessary, and then click the **Change** button.

2

16. Verify that Add or Remove Features is selected, as shown in Figure 2-3, and then click **Next**.

You could also use this applet to repair an installation of Office 2003 or remove it completely.

**TIP**

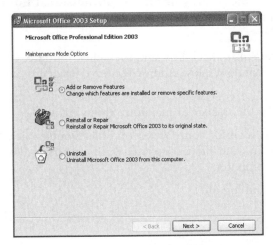

**Figure 2-3**   The Add or Remove Features option

17. Click to clear the **PowerPoint** check box, and then click **Update**.

18. Click **OK** to clear the success message. If you get an installation error, such as the one shown in Figure 2-4, insert the Office 2003 installation CD, and click **OK**. Click **OK** again in the Successful Update window.

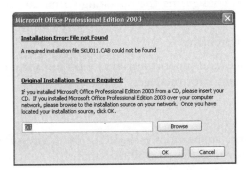

**Figure 2-4**   Installation error message for a missing CD

19. Close any open windows and programs. Click **Start**, **My Documents**. Note the difference in the icon for the PowerPoint file you created in Step 10. Double-click **My test of PowerPoint**. Read the error message. The OS no longer has any program installed that can open the PPT file. Click **Cancel**.

20. Minimize the My Documents window. Click **Start**, **Control Panel**, **Add or Remove Programs**. Insert the Microsoft Office 2003 installation CD, if necessary, and click **OK**. Click the **Microsoft Office (Professional Edition) 2003** item (your edition might vary) to highlight it, if necessary, and click the **Change** button. Click **Next**.

21. Click to select the **PowerPoint** check box, and then click **Update**. Click **OK** in the Successful Update window. Close Add or Remove Programs, and then close Control Panel.

22. Click **My Documents** in the taskbar to maximize the window.

23. Note the difference in the icon for your PowerPoint file. Double-click **My test of PowerPoint**. Again, your file is associated with a program (Power-Point) installed on your computer.

24. Close all open windows, and log off.

## Certification Objectives

Objectives for Microsoft Exam #70-272: Supporting Users and Troubleshooting Desktop Applications on a Microsoft Windows XP Operating System:

➤ Configure and troubleshoot Office applications.

➤ Answer end-user questions related to configuring Office applications.

➤ Customize folder settings.

➤ Answer end-user questions related to configuring the operating system to support an application.

➤ Troubleshoot application installation problems.

➤ Resolve issues related to Office application support features. Tasks include configuring Office applications and interpreting error messages.

## Review Questions

1. Which of the following are core applications included in the Microsoft Office 2003 Standard Edition retail version? (Choose all that apply.)
   a. Word
   b. Excel
   c. PowerPoint
   d. Access
   e. FrontPage

2. Which of the following are core applications included in the Microsoft Office 2003 Professional Edition retail version? (Choose all that apply.)

   a. Word

   b. Excel

   c. PowerPoint

   d. Access

   e. FrontPage

3. A file _____ is the component that associates a file with an application.

   a. name

   b. security

   c. extension

   d. attribute

4. To change the association of a file with an application, DSTs should choose which of the following options? (Choose all that apply.)

   a. Tools, File Associations, Change

   b. File, Associate, Change

   c. View, Details

   d. Tools, Folder Options, File Types, Change

5. Which of the following installation types are available for Office 2003? (Choose all that apply.)

   a. Typical

   b. Associate

   c. Minimal

   d. Full

# LAB 2.2 TROUBLESHOOTING OFFICE 2003 INSTALLATION PROBLEMS

## Objectives

The goal of this lab is to identify and describe techniques and tools for troubleshooting a failed installation of Office 2003.

## Materials Required

This lab requires the following:

➤ A computer running Microsoft Windows XP

➤ Internet access

Estimated completion time: 45 minutes

## Activity Background

Troubleshooting a failed installation of an application follows the same general rules or guidelines of troubleshooting any problem. Some of the tools you can use to troubleshoot a failed installation include the following:

➤ Your organization's knowledge base system, which might be help desk tracking software. Check to see whether the problem has happened before and what solution was used.

➤ Your own experiences installing the software. You might have run into this same problem previously and identified a solution that worked.

➤ The application software's installation instructions or manual.

➤ Any readme.txt files on the installation CD.

➤ For Microsoft Office installations, the Microsoft Web sites *www.microsoft.com/technet* and *http://support.microsoft.com*.

➤ The extensive Microsoft Knowledge Base (KB). It's unlikely that the problem you're having hasn't happened to someone else; chances are that Microsoft has documentation and potential solutions in its extensive Knowledge Base. Also, don't forget to check the Microsoft Office Web site at *http://office.microsoft.com*.

➤ Microsoft Resource Kits, another great tool for information. Although they aren't usually as comprehensive as the KB articles for troubleshooting, they do have documentation for installation and limited information on troubleshooting.

➤ Installation log files for error messages. Often, the error messages give you a clue about the reason for a failed installation.

For many students, the most useful tool is the Microsoft Knowledge Base, so you use it extensively in this lab to solve the following scenarios. Log pertinent information in the space provided. Use additional paper or a word processing document to supply details about your findings.

## ACTIVITY

**Scenario 1:** You are installing Microsoft Office 2003 for a user in your organization. The installation is a complete attended install. The setup process has been running for quite some time, but it doesn't finish, and eventually it fails. Another DST in your department tells you he's heard of some error logs that are created during an installation and says that sometimes you can figure out what went wrong by reviewing the files. When you ask the other DST what the names of the files are or where they are located, he replies that he has no idea. He had read about it in an online article and doesn't even remember what site it was.

What files is the DST referring to? What are the file names and where are they located? Include the source, if any, of your solution. Record your answer here.

_____

_____

_____

_____

_____

_____

**Scenario 2:** You're installing Microsoft Office 2003 for a user in your organization. The installation is a simple complete attended install. The setup process has been running for quite some time but suddenly quits. You don't get any error message, but the installation didn't finish.

What might be the cause of the problem, and what remedies could you try to solve it? Record your answer here. Include the source, if any, of your solution.

_____

_____

_____

_____

_____

_____

**Scenario 3:** You're installing Microsoft Office 2003 for a user in your organization. The installation is a simple complete attended install. You're using a standard CD install, not a network install. The setup process just doesn't seem to go past the initial window, and you notice that the CD drive is running constantly. You try putting your Toby Keith CD in the drive, and it plays fine.

What might be the cause of the problem, and what remedies could you try to solve it? Record your answer here. Include the source, if any, of your solution.

_____

_____

_____

_____

_____

_____

**Scenario 4:** You're installing Microsoft Office 2003 with a CD in an attended install. You get an error message saying "The Windows Installer service could not be accessed," and the installation stops.

What might be the cause of the problem, and what remedies could you try to solve it? Record your answer here. Include the source, if any, of your solution.

_____

_____

_____

_____

_____

_____

**Scenario 5:** All these attended installs are taking a lot of your time that you think would be better spent on other user support tasks. Your manager agrees with you and suggests that there must be a way to install Office 2003 without having to sit through every install. She asks you to research unattended installations of Office 2003 and would like your recommendations on whether it can be done and a quick overview of the process.

Where can you get information about unattended installations for the Microsoft Office 2003 suite? What information from your research would be pertinent for your manager's request for a quick overview of the process? Record your answer here. Include the source, if any, of your solution.

_____

_____

_____

_____

_____

## Certification Objectives

Objectives for Microsoft Exam #70-272: Supporting Users and Troubleshooting Desktop Applications on a Microsoft Windows XP Operating System:

➤ Answer end-user questions related to configuring the operating system to support an application.

➤ Troubleshoot application installation problems.

## Review Questions

1. Which of the following troubleshooting methods are appropriate in most circumstances? (Choose all that apply.)

   a. systematic approach

   b. hunt-and-peck approach

   c. divide-and-conquer approach

   d. shotgun approach

2. Which of the following actions might help resolve CD problems with an installation? (Choose all that apply.)

   a. Clean the CD.

   b. Replace with an undamaged CD.

   c. Turn on the CD autoplay feature.

   d. Check the BIOS settings and turn off enhanced BIOS features.

3. Which command-line tool can quickly tell you whether a CD is damaged?

   a. DIR /S

   b. FDISK /F

   c. SET CD=SYS

   d. CHKCD

4. The first step in the troubleshooting process is to _____ .

   a. define the problem

   b. hypothesize solutions

   c. gather information

   d. test solutions

5. The second step in the troubleshooting process is to _____ .

   a. define the problem

   b. hypothesize solutions

   c. gather information

   d. test solutions

# LAB 2.3 UNDERSTANDING OFFICE APPLICATION DEFAULT SETTINGS

## Objectives

The goal of this lab is to locate and identify some settings in several Microsoft Office 2003 applications.

## Materials Required

This lab requires the following:

➤    A computer running Microsoft Windows XP with Service Pack 1a

➤    Office 2003 installed

Estimated completion time: 30 minutes

## Activity Background

As you know, time is money. As you become familiar with the applications in the Office 2003 suite, you'll pick up favorite settings and options that make you more efficient and productive in your work. In this lab, you learn about just a few of the many available options.

**LAB ACTIVITY**

## ACTIVITY

1. Log on to a computer.

2. Click **Start**, point to **All Programs**, point to **Microsoft Office**, and click **Microsoft Office Word 2003**. Click **Cancel** if the Activation window opens.

If you have recently used Word 2003, you can simply open it from the Start menu.

**TIP**

3. In the new blank document, type your name, press **Enter**, type your address, press **Enter**, type your city, state, and ZIP code, and press **Enter**.

4. Click **Tools**, **Options** from the menu. (If you don't see Options as a choice, click the double down arrow at the bottom of the menu choices to see all the options.) Click the **View** tab, if necessary. In the Formatting marks section, click to select the **Spaces** and the **Paragraph marks** check boxes. Click **OK**.

5. View your document. Now each space you inserted is indicated by a small dot, and each hard carriage return (pressing the Enter key) is indicated with a paragraph mark. Repeat Step 4, but this time click to clear the **Spaces** and **Paragraph marks** check boxes (see Figure 2-5).

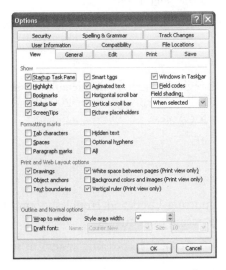

**Figure 2-5**   Removing paragraph marks and spaces

6. Click **Tools**, **Options** from the menu, and click the **View** tab, if necessary. Review the default settings.

7. Click the **General** tab, and review the options. Repeat this process for the **Edit** and **Print** tabs.

8. Click the **Save** tab. Notice that the default file save setting is a Word Document (*.doc) file. You could easily change the default file type to an HTML document for Web pages, but for now, leave the default setting as is. Click **Cancel** to close the Options dialog box without saving any changes.

9. Click **Tools**, **Options** from the menu, and click the **Spelling & Grammar** tab. Review the default settings and notice how Microsoft Word applies those settings. Click **Cancel**. Close Microsoft Word. Click **No** when prompted to save changes.

10. Click **Start**, point to **All Programs**, point to **Microsoft Office**, and click **Microsoft Office Excel 2003**. If necessary, close the Getting Started task pane.

11. Click **Tools**, **Options** from the menu. (If you don't see Options as a choice, click the double down arrow at the bottom of the menu choices to see all the options.) Click the **View** tab, if necessary. In the Window options section, click to clear the **Row & column headers** and the **Gridlines** check boxes. Click **OK**.

12. Notice that the spreadsheet now looks more like a word processing document than a spreadsheet. Users can quickly get in trouble playing with these options, and you'll be called on to "fix" the fruits of their labors. Repeat Step 11, but this time click to enable the **Row & column headers** and the **Gridlines** check boxes. Click **OK**. to return to the default settings.

13. Click **Tools**, **Options** from the menu, and review the options in the remaining tabs.

14. Close Excel without saving your work.

15. Using the same methods outlined previously, review the default settings for PowerPoint and Outlook. If you installed Microsoft Office 2003 Professional Edition, review the default settings for Access.

16. Close any open windows, and log off.

## Certification Objectives

Objectives for Microsoft Exam #70-272: Supporting Users and Troubleshooting Desktop Applications on a Microsoft Windows XP Operating System:

➤ Answer end-user questions related to configuring the operating system to support an application.

➤ Troubleshoot access to local resources.

➤ Answer end-user questions related to customizing the operating system to support an application.

➤ Answer end-user questions related to customizing Office applications.

➤ Resolve issues related to Office application support features. Tasks include configuring Office applications and interpreting error messages.

## Review Questions

1. The default file type setting for Microsoft Word 2003 is _____ .

   a. .txt

   b. .wpd

   c. .wps

   d. .doc

2. To change the default file location for saving a file in Microsoft Word 2003, which of the following series of actions would you take?

   a. File, Properties, Custom, and then modify the setting

   b. Tools, Options, File Locations, and then modify the setting

   c. Tools, Options, Save, and then modify the setting

   d. View, Document Map

3. To change the default file location for saving a file in Microsoft Excel 2003, which of the following tabs in the Options dialog box should you access?

   a. General

   b. Edit

   c. Save

   d. View

4. In Microsoft Excel 2003, how many sheets are configured by default for each new spreadsheet created?

   a. 1

   b. 2

   c. 3

   d. 4

5. How many default toolbars are available in Microsoft PowerPoint 2003?

   a. 1

   b. 5

   c. 10

   d. 20

## LAB 2.4 REVIEWING WINDOWS APPLICATIONS

### Objectives

The goal of this lab is to review several types of application programs that are installed by default with the Windows XP operating system.

### Materials Required

This lab requires the following:

➤ A computer running Windows XP with Service Pack 1a

➤ Administrative rights on the computer

➤ Internet access

Estimated completion time: 30 minutes

## Activity Background

Microsoft bundles many application programs with the Windows XP operating system. As a DST, you'll be required to help users with these applications. Many of these applications, such as Paint, Notepad, and WordPad, are simple or stripped-down tools that are easy to work with.

**LAB ACTIVITY**

### ACTIVITY

1. Log on to a computer. You need to be able to log on with administrative rights.

2. Click **Start**, point to **All Programs**, point to **Accessories**, and click **Notepad**. Notepad is a simple ASCII text editor that's good for typing short notes when you don't need the functions of a full-blown word processing program such as Word 2003. Type some text in Notepad. Click **File**, **Save** from the menu, and click the **Save as type** list arrow. Notice in Figure 2-6 that the only option is a basic .txt file type. Click **Cancel**. Also notice that no spell-check function is available in Notepad. Close Notepad, and click **No** to discard the changes.

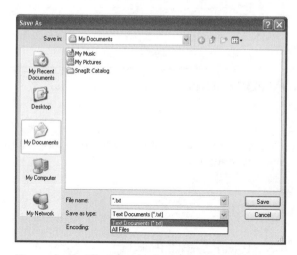

**Figure 2-6**    The Notepad Save As dialog box

3. Click **Start**, press the **Print Screen** key, point to **All Programs**, point to **Accessories**, and click **Paint**. Click **Edit**, **Paste** from the menu. You have captured a screen shot of your desktop and imported it into the Paint program.

4. In Paint, click **File**, **Save** from the menu, and then click the **Save as type** list arrow. You have several file type options, including JPEG, GIF, and PNG.

5. To change the file type, click **JPEG** in the list of options. Type **my screen print** in the File name text box, and click **Save**.

6. Click **File**, **Save As** from the menu, and click **256 Color Bitmap** in the Save as type list box. Ensure that **My Pictures** is selected in the Save in list box, and then type **my screen print** in the File name text box (if necessary). Click **Save**, and then click **Yes**. Close Paint.

7. Click **Start**, **My Pictures**, and then click **View**, **Details** from the menu. Notice the difference in file size between the .bmp format and the .jpg format. It's easy to see why .jpg is used so often on the Internet—it produces a much smaller file. Close all open windows.

8. Click **Start**, point to **All Programs**, point to **Accessories**, and click **Notepad**. (*Note:* If you have recently used Notepad, you can simply open it from the Start menu.) Type your name, and press **Enter**.

9. Click **Start**, point to **All Programs**, point to **Accessories**, point to **Accessibility**, and click **Magnifier**. Click **OK**.

10. Type your address, and press **Enter**. Resize the windows so that each window uses approximately one-half of your screen, as shown in Figure 2-7. When you have resized the two windows, they should look similar to Figure 2-8.

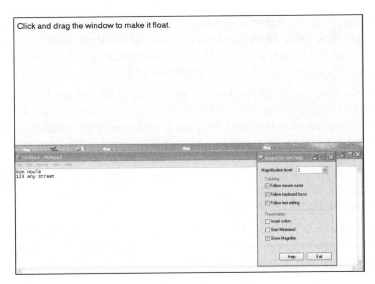

**Figure 2-7** Adjusting the Magnifier window

11. Observe how Magnifier works, and then click **Exit** to close Magnifier.

12. Click **File**, **Exit** from the menu, and then click **No** to close Notepad without saving the changes.

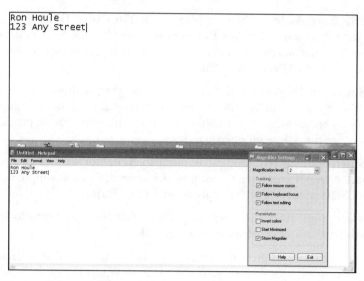

**Figure 2-8**    Magnifier working windows

13. Click **Start**, point to **All Programs**, point to **Accessories**, point to **System Tools**, and click **Disk Defragmenter**. Click the **Analyze** button to check whether your hard drive needs to be defragmented. When the analysis is finished, Disk Defragmenter displays a graphical analysis.

14. Review the color codes at the bottom of this window, and see how many files are stored in fragments on your drive. Fragmentation slows a computer's performance level because the hard drive must make more revolutions to gather one file from its many fragmented locations. Defragmentation can take some time, depending on the severity of the fragmentation. After it's started, it must be allowed to finish. When the analysis is finished, you see a status message that tells you whether you need to defragment your hard drive. Click the **View Report** button, if available.

15. View the report and notice the options available via the buttons at the bottom of Analysis Report dialog box: Print, Save As, Defragment, or Close. Close the Analysis Report dialog box and the Disk Defragmenter window.

**NOTE**    If you choose the Defragment option, be prepared to wait until the entire defragmentation has finished.

16. Explore and become familiar with other programs available in the Accessories menu. Try WordPad, Calculator, and others. Be prepared to cancel an operation if you aren't sure what it will do. Check the Help and Support Center for documentation to help you learn more about these programs. Close any remaining open windows.

17. Click **Start**, **Internet Explorer**. Click **Tools**, **Internet Options** from the Internet Explorer menu. Review the configuration options in the General tab, such as changing the home page, deleting cookies, and changing settings for temporary Internet files (see Figure 2-9). You'll be working with several of these settings in later chapters.

**Figure 2-9**   The Internet Options dialog box in Internet Explorer

18. In the Temporary Internet files section, click the **Settings** button. Notice how much space on your hard drive is reserved for caching copies of Web pages you have visited and the options to set when a Web page is reloaded.

19. Click **Cancel** in the Settings dialog box.

20. In the Internet Options dialog box, click the **Security** tab, and review the options. In this dialog box, you can add restricted sites to Internet Explorer (IE) or choose which sites you trust. Click the **Trusted sites** icon, and then click the **Sites** button. Type **https://thisismy70272classsecuretrustedsite.com** in the Add this Web site to the zone text box (see Figure 2-10), and click **Add**. Click **Cancel**.

**Figure 2-10**   Adding a trusted site

21. Review the other available tabs. You'll learn more about these options in subsequent chapters. Click **Cancel**.

22. Type **www.microsoft.com/technet** in the Address text box, and press **Enter**.

23. Type **home page setting** in the Search for text box and click **Knowledge Base** in the search location list (see Figure 2-11). Press **Enter** or click **Go**.

**Figure 2-11**   Search utility in TechNet

24. Review any Knowledge Base articles that might help you troubleshoot these settings.

25. Close Internet Explorer, and log off.

## Certification Objectives

Objectives for Microsoft Exam #70-272: Supporting Users and Troubleshooting Desktop Applications on a Microsoft Windows XP Operating System:

➤ Answer end-user questions related to configuring the operating system to support an application.

➤ Configure and troubleshoot Internet Explorer.

## Review Questions

1. If a user tells you her computer seems much slower than it used be and mentions that she's constantly saving and deleting files and does a lot of research on the Internet, which of the following tools could you use to give you clues about her computer's disk performance?

    a. General settings in Internet Explorer

    b. dxdiag

    c. Disk Defragmenter analyze tool

    d. Disk Defragmenter defragment tool

2. Which of the following are tabs available in the Internet Explorer Internet Options dialog box? (Choose all that apply.)

    a. Content

    b. Connections

    c. Availability

    d. Sites

3. Which of the following programs include a spell checking utility? (Choose all that apply.)

    a. Notepad

    b. Word 2003

    c. WordPad

    d. Edit

4. Which of the following tools could be used to create an image on your screen?

    a. System Tools

    b. Magnifier

    c. Disk Defragment

    d. Paint

5. Which of the following are installed by default with Windows XP? (Choose all that apply.)

   a. WordPad

   b. Photoshop

   c. Accessory Planner

   d. Paint

# CHAPTER THREE

# RESOLVE ISSUES RELATED TO CUSTOMIZING OPERATING SYSTEM SUPPORT APPLICATIONS

## Labs included in this chapter:

➤ Lab 3.1 Customizing the Taskbar
➤ Lab 3.2 Customizing Language Settings
➤ Lab 3.3 Changing Operating System Fonts
➤ Lab 3.4 Customizing Folder Settings

| Microsoft MCDST Exam #70-272 Objectives | |
|---|---|
| Objective | Lab |
| Resolve issues related to customizing the operating system to support applications. | 3.1, 3.2, 3.3, 3.4 |
| Answer end-user questions related to customizing the operating system to support an application. | 3.2, 3.3, 3.4 |
| Customize the Start menu and taskbar. | 3.1 |
| Customize regional settings. | 3.2 |
| Customize fonts. | 3.3 |
| Customize folder settings. | 3.4 |

## LAB 3.1 CUSTOMIZING THE TASKBAR

### Objectives

At the completion of this lab, you'll be able to answer questions to help users configure their Start menus and taskbars.

### Materials Required

This lab requires the following:

➤ A computer running Windows XP Professional with Service Pack 1a

Estimated completion time: 15 minutes

### Activity Background

The taskbar is one of the main interfaces to the Windows XP operating system. As a desktop support technician, often you'll be asked to help users configure their taskbars. Users might accidentally move their taskbars to a different area on the screen or want to know why their taskbars aren't always visible when running certain applications or programs. Working with the notification area of the taskbar is an essential skill for DSTs to master because this area supplies important information: the status of some of the computer applications running on this workstation.

In this activity, you work with the notification area of the taskbar and practice hiding and showing program icons that indicate an application's status. The notification area of the taskbar gives you a quick way to find out which mission-critical applications, such as antivirus and firewall software, are functioning.

LAB ACTIVITY

### ACTIVITY

1. Log on to a workstation running Windows XP Professional. You don't need administrative rights to perform any of the tasks in this lab.

2. Right-click a blank area on the taskbar next to the clock display. This area is called the notification area. Notice the options available on the shortcut menu.

3. Click the **Customize Notifications** option. You can use this dialog box to restore the defaults or select an icon listed under Current Items. For each icon, you have these display options: Hide when inactive, Always hide, or Always show. To see the icon for a program that has the Always hide option enabled, you click the Show hidden icons button at the far left of the notification area. Using the Hide when inactive option helps keep the notification area from becoming too crowded.

3

4. Click an icon in the Current Items list that has the Always show option enabled, and then click the down arrow in the Behavior column. (If you don't have an Always show option available, consult your instructor.) Click the **Always hide** option, and then click **OK**.

5. Observe that the icon has disappeared from the notification area of the taskbar. Click the **Show hidden icons** button to see the icon.

6. To return the icon to its original display state, right-click the notification area and click **Customize Notifications**. Click the icon you changed in Step 4 and in the Behavior column, click **Always show**. Click **OK**. You should see the icon displayed in the notification area again.

**NOTE**

To restore an icon to its original display status, you can also click the Restore Defaults button at the bottom of the Customize Notifications dialog box.

7. Close any open windows, and log off.

## Certification Objectives

Objectives for Microsoft Exam #70-272: Supporting Users and Troubleshooting Desktop Applications on a Microsoft Windows XP Operating System:

➤ Customize the Start menu and taskbar.

➤ Resolve issues related to customizing the operating system to support applications.

## Review Questions

1. Which of the following areas are found on the taskbar? (Choose all that apply.)
   a. notification area
   b. Languages icon
   c. Quick Launch area
   d. program area

2. Which of the following buttons is available in the Customize Notifications dialog box?
   a. Restore Defaults
   b. Regional Settings
   c. Fonts and Folders
   d. Show Start Menu

3. To display the clock in the taskbar's notification area, you should do which of the following?

    a. Deselect the Show the clock option in the Taskbar and Start Menu Properties dialog box.

    b. Select the Show the clock option in the Taskbar and Start Menu Properties dialog box.

    c. Select Show time in the Regional Settings and Time dialog box.

    d. Enter Show Time from the command prompt.

4. To customize the taskbar's notification area, which of the following methods should you use? (Choose two answers.)

    a. Right-click the notification area and select Customize Notifications from the menu.

    b. Right-click any blank area of the taskbar and select Customize Notifications from the menu.

    c. Right-click the desktop and select Customize Notifications from the menu.

    d. Click Customize in the Taskbar and Start Menu Properties dialog box.

5. What option is available when configuring the display of items in the notification area?

    a. Hide when inactive

    b. Network Resources

    c. Customize Settings

    d. Customize Application

# LAB 3.2 CUSTOMIZING LANGUAGE SETTINGS

## Objectives

After completing this lab, you will be able to customize regional settings for languages other than English and assist users in making these configuration changes to their workstations.

## Materials Required

This lab requires the following:

➤ A computer running Windows XP Professional with Service Pack 1a and Microsoft Office 2003 Suite

3

Estimated completion time: 25 minutes

## Activity Background

Many companies have offices located in different parts of the world. As a DST, you might be required to support users in configuring multiple languages, currencies, and date formats. For example, Europeans do not use the same format for their dates that Americans do. The date January 21, 2004 is written as 21 January 2004 in most European countries. You might also need to answer questions about adding language support to users' workstations. In this activity, you practice adding another language on your workstation so that you can accommodate clients working in offices located in Japan.

## ACTIVITY

1. Log on to a workstation running Windows XP Professional. You don't need administrative rights to perform any of the tasks in this lab.

2. Click **Start**, **Control Panel**, and then click **Date, Time, Language, and Regional Options** in the Pick a category window. (You might need to click Switch to Category View before you see the Pick a category window.) In the Date, Time, Language, and Regional Options window, click **Regional and Language Options** to open the Regional and Language Options dialog box, shown in Figure 3-1.

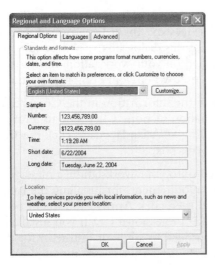

**Figure 3-1**   The Regional and Language Options dialog box

3. Click the **Regional Options** tab (if necessary), and review the options available for formatting numbers, currency, time, and date. Click the **Customize** button to open the Customize Regional Options dialog box, shown in Figure 3-2 (note that your entries in the figure might differ) and review the customization options. When you're done, click **Cancel** to return to the Regional Options tab.

**Figure 3-2**   Customizing regional number options

4. Click the **Languages** tab and review the available options. Next, click the **Details** button to open the Text Services and Input Languages dialog box, shown in Figure 3-3. The contents of this dialog box vary depending on which languages are currently installed on your workstation. In this dialog box, you select the default language used when your computer starts.

5. Click the **Advanced** tab and review the information in the Compatibility Configuration and System Configuration sections. Click **OK** to return to the Languages tab. Because you're installing an Asian language, click the **Install files for East Asian languages** check box.

6. Before the necessary files are copied onto your workstation, a message box is displayed to notify you of the space requirements for installing the language files (see Figure 3-4). Click **OK**, and then click **Apply**. You might be prompted to insert your Windows XP Professional CD. If you installed Windows XP from a network server, you need to ask your instructor for the location of the files needed to complete the lab. After several minutes, you're prompted to restart your workstation. Click **Yes** and then remove the CD from the CD drive.

3

**Figure 3-3**    Selecting a default language in the Text Services and Input Languages dialog box

**Figure 3-4**    The memory requirement message box for Asian languages

7. After your workstation restarts, repeat Step 2, if necessary. Click the **Regional Options** tab (if necessary), click the list arrow in the Standards and formats section, and click **Japanese** in the list of options. Note the changes in the samples listed in this tab. Click the **EN** icon on the Language bar, and then click **JP (Japanese)** on the shortcut menu. Click the **JP** icon and note several new icons that appear on your taskbar. Click the **(Input Mode)** icon (hold your mouse pointer over the icons to find the correct one), and then click the **Hiragana** option. (*Note*: Hiragana is one of the written Japanese languages.)

8. You have just installed and configured your workstation to write Japanese characters and to change the way dates, currency, numbers, and time are formatted. To change back to English, click the **JP** on the Language bar, and click **EN English (United States)**.

9. Close any open windows, and log off

## Certification Objectives

Objectives for Microsoft Exam #70-272: Supporting Users and Troubleshooting Desktop Applications on a Microsoft Windows XP Operating System:

➤ Answer end-user questions related to configuring the operating system to support an application.

➤ Customize regional settings.

➤ Resolve issues related to customizing the operating system to support applications.

## Review Questions

1. Which of the following methods should you use to make sure a user can write Japanese characters in her Microsoft Word 2003 document?

   a. Verify that her workstation has a copy of Microsoft Word for Japanese.

   b. Configure her workstation for multiple language support by using Regedt32.

   c. Verify that the input locale for Japanese has been configured on her workstation.

   d. Do nothing. (Japanese characters are available to users by default.)

2. To select French as the default language when using the Spelling and Grammar utility in Microsoft Word 2003 on a workstation configured with multiple languages, you should do which of the following?

   a. Select France as the default locale in the Regional and Language Options dialog box.

   b. Select France as the default locale in the Microsoft Word 2003 Language Options dialog box.

   c. Click Tools, Language, Set Language and select French (France) in the Language dialog box in Microsoft Word 2003. Finally, click the Default button.

   d. Select France as the default locale in the Foreign Country Languages dialog box.

3. To configure a workstation running Windows XP Professional to display Asian language characters in Windows Office 2003 products, you should do which of the following?

   a. Select Install files for East Asian languages in the Languages tab of the Regional and Language Options dialog box.

   b. Select Install files for East Asian languages in the Regional Options tab of the Regional and Language Options dialog box.

3

   c. Select Install files for East Asian languages in the Advanced tab of the Regional and Language Options dialog box.

   d. Select Install files for East Asian languages in the General tab of the Regional and Language Options dialog box.

4. To add the Language bar to your workstation running Windows XP Professional, you should do which of the following?

   a. Right-click the taskbar and select Language Bar from the menu.

   b. Right-click the taskbar, select Toolbars, and then select Language Bar from the menu.

   c. Right-click the desktop and select Language Bar from the menu.

   d. Click Customize in the Taskbar and Start Menu Properties dialog box.

5. To select Japanese as the default language to use when you start your computer, you should do which of the following?

   a. Select Japanese in the Settings tab of the Text Services and Input Languages dialog box.

   b. Select Japanese in the Regional and Language Options dialog box.

   c. Select Japanese in the Advanced tab of the Regional and Language Options dialog box.

   d. Select Japanese in the Languages tab of the Regional and Language Options dialog box.

## LAB 3.3 CHANGING OPERATING SYSTEM FONTS

### Objectives

After completing this lab, you will be able to change the default fonts on workstations running Windows XP Professional. You'll also be able to select different font sizes, enabling your users to have the freedom to select larger font sizes for more comfortable reading.

### Materials Required

This lab requires the following:

➤ A computer running Windows XP Professional with Service Pack 1a and Microsoft Office 2003

Estimated completion time: 15 minutes

## Activity Background

As a DST, you might be asked to change the default font on a workstation running Windows XP Professional. Users might require a larger font or different background colors for better readability, for example. In this activity, you practice changing the default font to make it easier for a user having difficulty reading the small fonts used in an application.

### ACTIVITY

LAB ACTIVITY

1. Log on to a workstation running Windows XP Professional.

2. Right-click a blank area on your desktop and click **Properties**. In the Display Properties dialog box, click the **Appearance** tab. Click the **Font size** list arrow, and then click **Extra Large Fonts** in the list of options. Click the **OK** button. Click the **Start** button to see a noticeable difference in the font size of menu selections.

3. To see how this change has affected Office 2003 products, open Microsoft Word 2003 and note the menu options at the top of the screen. Click **File** and notice the change in the size of the menu font.

4. Close Microsoft Word.

5. Open Microsoft Excel 2003 and note the menu options at the top of the screen. Write down all the areas in the Microsoft Excel spreadsheet where you see larger font sizes and any areas where you don't notice a change in font size.

6. Close Microsoft Excel.

7. Open Microsoft Outlook 2003 and note any changes in font size. You should also see a considerable difference in the Outlook Shortcuts and Folder list. Changing the font size in the Windows XP operating system has affected all Microsoft Office 2003 applications.

8. Close Microsoft Outlook.

9. To change the font size back to its default setting, click **Start**, **Control Panel**, and then double-click **Display**. (You might need to click Switch to Classic View before you can double-click Display.) Click the **Appearance** tab (if necessary), click the **Font size** list arrow, and click **Normal** in the list of options. Click **Apply**. Time permitting, explore the other tabs in the dialog box. When you're done, click **OK**.

10. Open Microsoft Word and notice that the menu options have returned to the original font size.

11. Close Microsoft Word. Close any open windows, and log off.

## Certification Objectives

Objectives for Microsoft Exam #70-272: Supporting Users and Troubleshooting Desktop Applications on a Microsoft Windows XP Operating System:

➤ Answer end-user questions related to configuring the operating system to support an application.

➤ Customize fonts.

➤ Resolve issues related to customizing the operating system to support applications.

## Review Questions

1. Which of the following options for font size is available in the Appearance tab of the Display Properties dialog box? (Choose all that apply.)

    a. Big Fonts

    b. Normal Fonts

    c. Large Fonts

    d. Extra Large Fonts

    e. Small Fonts

2. Which of the following is a theme in the Display Properties dialog box?

    a. Screen

    b. Regional

    c. Windows XP

    d. Standard Display

3. To display larger fonts for a user having difficulty reading the standard font size, you should do which of the following?

    a. Select Large Fonts in the Appearance tab of the Display Properties dialog box.

    b. Select Big Fonts in the Appearance tab of the Display Properties dialog box.

    c. Select Large Fonts in the Settings tab of the Display Properties dialog box.

    d. Select Large Fonts in the Desktop tab of the Display Properties dialog box.

4. Changing the font size in the Display Properties dialog box changes the font size for which of the following?

    a. only Windows XP Professional

    b. only Microsoft word processing applications

c. all Microsoft Office Suite products

d. only selected Microsoft Office Suite products

5. Which of the following methods do you use to open the Display Properties dialog box? (Choose two answers.)

a. Right-click the taskbar and select Properties.

b. Right-click the desktop and select Properties.

c. Click Start, Control Panel, Appearance and Themes, Display.

d. Click Start, Display Properties.

---

# LAB 3.4 CUSTOMIZING FOLDER SETTINGS

## Objectives

After completing this lab, you will be able to customize folder settings for workstations running Windows XP Professional.

## Materials Required

This lab requires the following:

➤ A computer running Windows XP Professional with Service Pack 1a

Estimated completion time: 20 minutes

## Activity Background

As a DST, you might be asked to change the default folder options on workstations running Windows XP Professional. Users might want folders that have encrypted or compressed files displayed in a different color, for example, or have trouble copying and moving folders. In this activity, you practice changing display options so that users can use the click-and-drag method to move the contents of one folder to another. You also change folder attributes to use different display colors so that users can quickly determine whether a folder contains compressed data.

LAB ACTIVITY

## ACTIVITY

1. Log on to a workstation running Windows XP Professional.

2. Right-click the **Start** button and click **Explore**. Click **Local Disk (C:)**. From the menu, click **File**, point to **New**, and click **Folder**. Backspace to delete the text NewFolder, and type your name for this new folder. Right-click the folder you created, and click **Properties**. In the **Properties** dialog

box, click the **Advanced** button to open the Advanced Attributes dialog box, shown in Figure 3-5.

3. Click the **Compress contents to save disk space** check box, as shown in Figure 3-5, and click **OK**. Any files copied into this folder will be compressed. Later in this lab, you see how the folder can be displayed in a different color to make it easier to know which folders have compression enabled.

**Figure 3-5** Configuring the Compress attribute

4. Click **OK** to close the Properties dialog box.

5. To make it possible for a user to view each folder in its own window, right-click the **Start** button and click **Explore** to open Windows Explorer, if necessary. Click **Tools**, **Folder Options** from the menu. Click the **General** tab (if necessary), and note the available options. You can use the Restore Defaults button if a user doesn't want certain configuration changes you've made, such as altering the number of mouse clicks needed to open an item.

6. In the Browse folders section, click the **Open each folder in its own window** option button (see Figure 3-6). Click **Apply**. With this option enabled, users can click and drag folders.

7. Click the **View** tab. You use this tab for most changes to folder settings. Scroll down the **Advanced settings** section to view all the available configuration settings. For most users, you should verify that the Hide protected operating system files (Recommended) option is selected. This option can help prevent users from accidentally deleting important system files from their workstations. If they can't see it, they probably won't delete it!

8. Scroll down the list, click the **Show encrypted or compressed NTFS files in color** option, if necessary, and then click **Apply**.

9. Click the **File Types** tab. You use this tab to establish file associations for programs. In other words, you can configure file associations so that if you click a file attachment with a .doc extension, the file is automatically opened in Microsoft Office Word. In the Registered file types list, click **DOC** in the Extensions column. Note the information displayed in the Details section at

**Figure 3-6**    Selecting the option to open a folder in its own window

the bottom (see Figure 3-7). If you want to change this association, you simply click the Change button and choose a different application to open a file with a .doc extension.

**Figure 3-7**    Changing a file association

10.  Click the **Offline Files** tab. If your workstation has Fast User Switching enabled, you see the message shown in Figure 3-8. Fast User Switching makes it possible to switch between multiple users logged on to a workstation without having to log off. This feature prevents users from using the Offline Files

option, however. Take some time to review the other settings available in the Folder Options dialog box. When you're done, close all open windows, and log off.

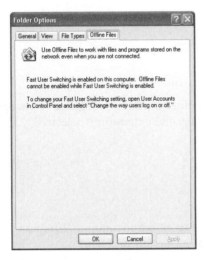

**Figure 3-8**   The Fast User Switching option has been enabled

## Certification Objectives

Objectives for Microsoft Exam #70-272: Supporting Users and Troubleshooting Desktop Applications on a Microsoft Windows XP Operating System:

➤ Answer end-user questions related to configuring the operating system to support an application.

➤ Customize folder settings.

➤ Resolve issues related to customizing the operating system to support applications.

## Review Questions

1. Which of the following folder options prevents users from knowing whether an e-mail attachment is a Microsoft Word document, not a script file?

    a. Show hidden files and folders

    b. Hide filename extensions

    c. Hide operating system files

    d. Hide scripts

2. A user wants to click and drag the contents of one folder to another folder, but each time he clicks the child folder, he can't view the folder he wants to drag to. What option would you choose in the Folder Options dialog box to solve this problem?

   a. Open each folder in the same window

   b. Open each folder in its own window

   c. Open each folder separately

   d. Open each folder in a different window

3. Which tab would you select in the Folder Options dialog box to change the application that opens when a particular file extension is selected?

   a. General

   b. View

   c. File Extensions

   d. File Types

4. A user can't access offline files on her workstation running Windows XP Professional. What is the most likely reason for this problem?

   a. The workstation is not connected to the Internet.

   b. The workstation has multiple hard disks.

   c. The workstation is formatted with NTFS partitions.

   d. Fast User Switching is enabled on the workstation.

5. A user wants an easy way to tell whether the contents of a folder have been compressed. What option would you set to solve this problem?

   a. In the View tab of the Folder Options dialog box, select Show encrypted or compressed NTFS files in color.

   b. In the General tab of the Folder Options dialog box, select Show encrypted or compressed NTFS files in color.

   c. In the Advanced tab of the Folder Options dialog box, select Show encrypted or compressed NTFS files in color.

   d. In the File Types tab of the Folder Options dialog box, select Show encrypted or compressed NTFS files in color.

# CONFIGURE USER RELATED ISSUES

---

## Labs included in this chapter:

➤ Exploring User Accounts

➤ Working with the Start Menu

➤ Working with File Extensions

➤ Creating an Error Report

---

| Microsoft MCDST Exam #70-272 Objectives |
|---|
| **Objective** |
| Although the labs in this chapter pertain to knowledge and skills desktop support technicians should have to fulfill their job responsibilities, they don't map directly to any MCDST certification objectives. |

## Lab 4.1 Exploring User Accounts

### Objectives

The goal of this lab is to understand the basic process of building user accounts. In addition, you explore what can be done with the two different types of accounts. By having a thorough understanding of the differences, you can help end users when they have questions about why they can—or cannot—do something on their accounts.

### Materials Required

This lab requires the following:

➤ A computer running Microsoft Windows XP

➤ Administrative rights on the computer

Estimated completion time: 10 minutes

### Activity Background

In a busy office or other work environment, you'll likely have multiple user accounts on a single machine. Each basic account has administrative or limited rights. An account with administrative rights is more powerful than one with only limited rights, as you will see in this activity. You'll find that different users need different levels of rights, depending on their job descriptions in your organization. Although others decide the level of rights, often it's up to you to set up user accounts to match those rights.

**LAB ACTIVITY**

### Activity

1. Log on to the computer. You need to be able to log on with administrative rights.

2. Click **Start**, **Control Panel**. If necessary, click **Switch to Classic View**, and then double-click **User Accounts**. Click the **Create a new account** link. Your screen should resemble Figure 4-1. Type **Test Account #1** in the Type a name for the new account text box, and then click **Next**.

3. Click the **Computer administrator** option button, if necessary, and then click the **Create Account** button.

4. Click the **Create a new account** link, type **Test Account #2** in the Type a name for the new account text box, and then click **Next**.

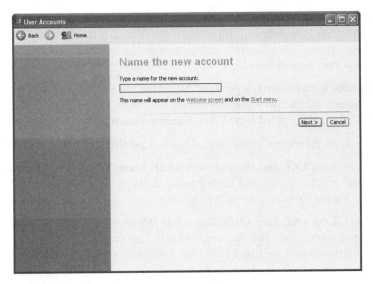

**Figure 4-1**   The User Account window

5. Click the **Limited** option button, as shown in Figure 4-2, and then click **Create Account**.

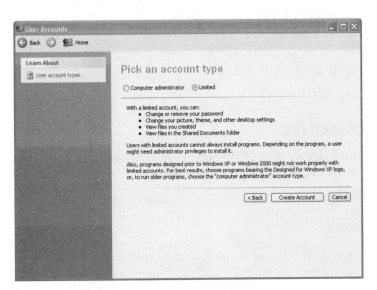

**Figure 4-2**   Choosing a different account type

6. Close the User Accounts window, and then close the Control Panel window.

7. Click **Start**, **Log Off**, and then click **Switch User**. Click **Test Account #2**. Wait while XP loads the settings for this account.

8. Click **Start**, **Control Panel**, and then click **User Accounts**. Note that you do not have links for deleting other accounts. These links do not exist because you are signed in with a limited account. In fact, you can see only the account with which you signed in.

9. Click **Create a password**, type **Test Account #2** in the first text box, type **Test Account #2** in the second text box, and then type a password hint of your choosing in the third box. Click **Create Password**.

10. Close the User Accounts window, and then close the Control Panel window.

11. Click **Start**, **Log Off**, and then click **Switch User**. Click **Test Account #2**. Notice that you are prompted for a password. Type **Test Account #2**, and then press **Enter**. You return to the desktop.

12. Click **Start**, **Log Off**, **Log Off**. Wait while Windows XP logs you off. Notice in the logon screen that Test Account #1 and Test Account #2 are both listed. Other accounts might be listed based on how your computer has been used before.

13. Click **Test Account #1**. Click **Start**, **Control Panel**, and then click **User Accounts**. Note that you can see other accounts now because you are signed in with an Administrator account.

14. Click **Test Account #2**, and then click **Delete the account**. Click **Delete Files**, and then click **Delete Account**. Note that your current account allowed you to make this deletion, even though the account to be deleted was password protected.

15. Close all open windows.

16. Log off from Test Account #1.

## Certification Objectives

Objectives for Microsoft Exam #70–272: Supporting Users and Troubleshooting Desktop Applications on a Microsoft Windows XP Operating System:

➤ None—Informational only

## Review Questions

1. If you're logged on using an account with administrative rights, you can switch to an account with limited rights without logging off first. True or False?

2. Fast User Switching is not available on a computer when that computer is part of a _____ .

3. Because it's paired with the Administrator account, the Guest account in Windows XP is enabled by default. True or False?

4. If your computer has only one account, what do you know about that account?

    a. It is a limited account.

    b. It is the Guest account.

    c. It must be a computer administrator account.

    d. It must be paired with a Guest account.

5. A limited account in Windows XP can change the picture associated with the Guest account. True or False?

**4**

## LAB 4.2 WORKING WITH THE START MENU

### Objectives

The goal of this lab is to understand the effects of user actions on the Start menu. This knowledge will help you guide users when they ask why one user sees a particular item on his Start menu but another user, who might use the same computer but during a different work shift and with a different account, can't see the same elements on her Start menu.

### Materials Required

This lab requires the following:

➤ A computer running Microsoft Windows XP

➤ Administrative rights on the computer

➤ Completion of Lab 4.1

Estimated completion time: 15 minutes

### Activity Background

The Start menu contains the elements that users access frequently. Whether the elements are there because of a user's high-frequency activity or because they were pinned, the end result is a Start menu that quickly becomes unique for each account user on the computer.

LAB ACTIVITY

### ACTIVITY

1. Log on to the computer. You need to be able to log on with administrative rights.

2. Click **Start**, **Control Panel**, and click **User Accounts**.

3. Click **Create a new account**, type **Test Account #2** in the Type a name for the new account text box, and then click **Next**.

4. Click the **Computer administrator** option button, if necessary, and then click **Create Account**.

5. Close the User Accounts window, and then close the Control Panel window.

6. Click **Start**, **Log Off**, **Log Off**.

7. Click **Test Account #1**. Wait while the personal settings are loaded. Click **Start** and notice the order of programs on the Start menu on the left side of your screen. Notice that Notepad is not listed on the Start menu.

8. Click **Start**, if necessary, point to **All Programs**, point to **Accessories**, and then click **Notepad**. Close the Notepad window.

9. Click **Start** and notice the order of programs on the Start menu. Notice that Notepad has moved into the bottom position on the Start menu.

**NOTE**

If you have more than the default programs on the Start menu, Notepad might not appear until you open it a few more times.

10. Repeat Step 8 three times.

11. Click **Start** and notice the order of programs on the Start menu. Notice that Notepad has moved up in its position on the Start menu.

12. Click **Start**, **Log Off**, **Log Off**.

13. Click **Test Account #2**. Wait while the personal settings are loaded. Click **Start** and notice the order of programs on the Start menu. Notice that Notepad is not listed on the Start menu.

14. Repeat Step 8 three times, except replace WordPad for Notepad.

15. Click **Start** and notice the order of programs on the Start menu. Notice that WordPad is now listed on the Start menu.

16. Repeat Step 8 four times, except replace Paint for WordPad.

17. Click **Start** and notice the order of programs on the Start menu. Notice that Paint is now listed on the Start menu in a higher position than WordPad.

18. Drag the Paint icon from its current location to a position above the separator bar on the Start menu, as shown in Figure 4-3.

19. Click **Start** (if necessary), **Log Off**, **Log Off**.

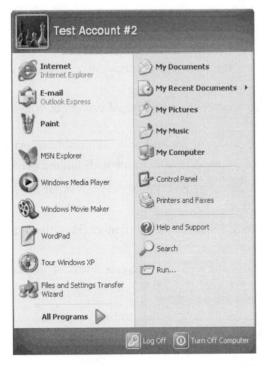

**Figure 4-3**   Paint has been moved above the separator bar

20. Click **Test Account #1**. Wait while the personal settings are loaded. Click **Start** and notice the order of programs on the Start menu. Notice that WordPad is not listed on the Start menu and neither is Paint. The two accounts—Test Account #1 and Test Account #2—don't directly affect each other's Start menu. Right-click **Notepad**, and then click **Pin to Start menu**. Notice that this action had the same effect as the dragging action did for Test Account #2.

21. Log off Test Account #1 and log on to Test Account #2. Note that the Start menu for this account hasn't changed, even though you pinned an item in the Start menu for Test Account #1.

22. Log off Test Account #2.

## Certification Objectives

Objectives for Microsoft Exam #70-272: Supporting Users and Troubleshooting Desktop Applications on a Microsoft Windows XP Operating System:

➤ None—Informational only

## Review Questions

1. You can unpin items from the Classic Start menu. True or False?

2. You can be logged on to two accounts with administrative privileges at the same time. True or False?

3. When you are logged on to an account with limited privileges, which of the following statements is true?

    a. You can also be logged on to an account with administrative privileges.

    b. You can also be logged on to another account with limited privileges.

    c. You can also be logged on to an account with Guest privileges.

    d. None of the above is true.

4. You can unpin an item from the Start menu by right-clicking the item and then clicking _____ .

5. Items on the Start menu above the separator line can always be unpinned. True or False?

## LAB 4.3 WORKING WITH FILE EXTENSIONS

### Objectives

The goal of this lab is to understand how file extensions help Windows XP select the correct program to open a particular file. Armed with a knowledge of these file extensions, you'll become efficient at helping end users who want to open files quickly and easily.

### Materials Required

This lab requires the following:

➤ A computer running Microsoft Windows XP

➤ Administrative rights on the computer

Estimated completion time:  10 minutes

### Activity Background

In Windows XP, a file extension helps identify the type of file. When you change the program associated with a file extension, you are changing that association for all instances of that file type. You can use a shortcut menu option, however, to override the association.

## Activity Background

Programs can freeze unexpectedly in Windows XP. Whether it's a simple program, such as Notepad, or a complicated program, such as one of the programs in the Office suite, the end result is the same: The program stops and Windows XP tries, by default, to generate an error report to send to Microsoft. In this activity, you get a chance to view the basic contents of an error report.

### ACTIVITY

1. Log on to Test Account #1.

2. Click **Start**, **My Music**, and double-click **Sample Music**. Right-click the New Stories (Highway Blues) icon, click **Open With**, and then click **Notepad**. Click **OK**.

3. Click in the text in the Notepad window, if necessary, press **Ctrl+A**, and then click **Format**, **Font** from the menu.

4. In the Font list box, click **MS Sans Serif**, and in the Font style list box, click **Bold Italic**. In the Size text box, type **72**, and then click **OK**. Click **Format**, **Word Wrap** from the menu.

5. Click **File**, **Save As** from the menu. Click **Desktop** in the Save in list box, and then click **Save**.

6. Immediately and repeatedly click the **Close** button at the top-right corner of the Notepad window. After a few seconds, Notepad stops responding and displays a message box advising you of that fact, as shown in Figure 4-5. Click **End Now**.

**Figure 4-5**    Program has stopped running

7. In the message box that opens, click the **click here** link. Your screen should resemble Figure 4-6.

8. Read the reporting details, and then click the first **click here** link. Read the technical details in the resulting Error Report Contents message window.

### ACTIVITY

1. Log on to the computer. You need to be able to log on with administrative rights.

2. Right-click **Start**, and then click **Explore**.

3. Click **Tools**, **Folder Options** from the menu. Your screen should resemble Figure 4-4.

**Figure 4-4**    The Folder Options dialog box

4. Click the **File Types** tab. In the Registered file types list box, scroll down to and click the **TXT Text Document** entry. At the bottom of the dialog box, note that Windows XP uses Notepad, by default, to open files with the .txt file extension.

5. Click **Cancel**, and then close Windows Explorer.

6. Click **Start**, point to **All Programs**, point to **Accessories**, and then click **Notepad**. Type **File Extension Test**, and then click **File**, **Save As** from the menu. Click **Desktop** in the Save in list box, type **Test Document** in the File name text box, and then click **Save**. Close the Notepad window.

7. On your desktop, double-click the **Test Document** icon. Notice that Windows XP automatically opens the document in Notepad. Close Notepad.

8. Right-click **Start**, and then click **Explore**.

9. Click **Tools**, **Folder Options** from the menu.

10. Click the **File Types** tab. In the Registered file types list box, scroll down to and click the **TXT Text Document** entry. At the bottom of the dialog box, note that Windows XP still uses Notepad, by default, to open files with the .txt file extension.

11. Click the **Change** button, click **Internet Explorer** in the Open With dialog box, and then click **OK**. At the bottom of the Folder Options dialog box, note that Windows XP will now use Internet Explorer to open files with this file extension.

12. Click **Close**, and then close Windows Explorer.

13. On your desktop, double-click the **Test Document** icon. Notice that Windows XP automatically opens the document in Internet Explorer.

14. Close the Internet Explorer window. Right-click the **Test Document** icon, point to **Open With**, and then click **Notepad**. The file opens in Notepad because your choice on the menu overrode the file extension setting.

15. Close Notepad.

16. Repeat Steps 8 to 12, but this time, change the setting back to Notepad.

17. Log off your account.

## Certification Objectives

Objectives for Microsoft Exam #70-272: Supporting Users and Troubleshooting Desktop Applications on a Microsoft Windows XP Operating System:

➤ None—Informational only

## Review Questions

1. By default, you can open an item in Windows XP with a single click. You can change that option to a double-click by accessing the _____ tab in the Folder Options dialog box.

   a. File Types

   b. File View

   c. View

   d. General

2. By default for an Administrator account, which of the following is not a tab the Folder Options dialog box?

   a. Offline File

   b. File Types

   c. View

   d. Settings

3. You use the _____ tab in the Folder Options dialog box to change file extension associations.

4. By default, not all extensions in Windows XP have an associated program. True or False?

5. You can click the _____ button in the Folder Options dialog box to access options such as the Confirm open after download and Always show extension check boxes.

## LAB 4.4 CREATING AN ERROR REPORT

### Objectives

The goal of this lab is to recognize when a program has stopped working correctly and learn the steps Windows XP takes to handle this situation so that you can help end users who might be frustrated with a nonresponsive (or hung) program.

### Materials Required

This lab requires the following:

➤ A computer running Microsoft Windows XP

➤ Administrative rights on the computer

➤ Completion of Lab 4.1

Estimated completion time: 15 minutes

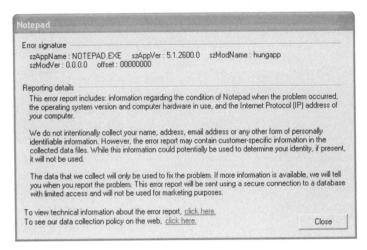

**Figure 4-6**  Error information

9. Click **Close**, click **Close** again, and then click the **Don't Send** button.

10. Log off Test Account #1.

## Certification Objectives

Objectives for Microsoft Exam #70-272: Supporting Users and Troubleshooting Desktop Applications on a Microsoft Windows XP Operating System:

➤ None—Informational only

## Review Questions

1. Notepad can be used to open files other than those with the .txt file extension. True or False?

2. You can access Error Reporting options via the _____ tab of the System Properties dialog box.

3. To send an error report to Microsoft, your computer must have Internet access and encryption capabilities enabled by default. True or False?

4. Which of the following is *not* normally included in the reporting details of an error report in Windows XP?

   a. condition of the program when the problem occurred

   b. the hardware in use

   c. the IP address of your computer

   d. the space left on your hard drive

5. The content of various files on your system can be included with an error report that's sent to Microsoft. True or False?

**ACTIVITY**

1. Log on to the computer. You need to be able to log on with administrative rights.

2. Right-click **Start**, and then click **Explore**.

3. Click **Tools**, **Folder Options** from the menu. Your screen should resemble Figure 4-4.

**4**

**Figure 4-4**   The Folder Options dialog box

4. Click the **File Types** tab. In the Registered file types list box, scroll down to and click the **TXT Text Document** entry. At the bottom of the dialog box, note that Windows XP uses Notepad, by default, to open files with the .txt file extension.

5. Click **Cancel**, and then close Windows Explorer.

6. Click **Start**, point to **All Programs**, point to **Accessories**, and then click **Notepad**. Type **File Extension Test**, and then click **File**, **Save As** from the menu. Click **Desktop** in the Save in list box, type **Test Document** in the File name text box, and then click **Save**. Close the Notepad window.

7. On your desktop, double-click the **Test Document** icon. Notice that Windows XP automatically opens the document in Notepad. Close Notepad.

8. Right-click **Start**, and then click **Explore**.

9. Click **Tools**, **Folder Options** from the menu.

10. Click the **File Types** tab. In the Registered file types list box, scroll down to and click the **TXT Text Document** entry. At the bottom of the dialog box, note that Windows XP still uses Notepad, by default, to open files with the .txt file extension.

11. Click the **Change** button, click **Internet Explorer** in the Open With dialog box, and then click **OK**. At the bottom of the Folder Options dialog box, note that Windows XP will now use Internet Explorer to open files with this file extension.

12. Click **Close**, and then close Windows Explorer.

13. On your desktop, double-click the **Test Document** icon. Notice that Windows XP automatically opens the document in Internet Explorer.

14. Close the Internet Explorer window. Right-click the **Test Document** icon, point to **Open With**, and then click **Notepad**. The file opens in Notepad because your choice on the menu overrode the file extension setting.

15. Close Notepad.

16. Repeat Steps 8 to 12, but this time, change the setting back to Notepad.

17. Log off your account.

## Certification Objectives

Objectives for Microsoft Exam #70-272: Supporting Users and Troubleshooting Desktop Applications on a Microsoft Windows XP Operating System:

➤ None—Informational only

## Review Questions

1. By default, you can open an item in Windows XP with a single click. You can change that option to a double-click by accessing the _____ tab in the Folder Options dialog box.

   a. File Types

   b. File View

   c. View

   d. General

2. By default for an Administrator account, which of the following is not a tab in the Folder Options dialog box?

    a. Offline File

    b. File Types

    c. View

    d. Settings

3. You use the _____ tab in the Folder Options dialog box to change file extension associations.

4. By default, not all extensions in Windows XP have an associated program. True or False?

5. You can click the _____ button in the Folder Options dialog box to access options such as the Confirm open after download and Always show extension check boxes.

# LAB 4.4 CREATING AN ERROR REPORT

## Objectives

The goal of this lab is to recognize when a program has stopped working correctly and learn the steps Windows XP takes to handle this situation so that you can help end users who might be frustrated with a nonresponsive (or hung) program.

## Materials Required

This lab requires the following:

➤ A computer running Microsoft Windows XP

➤ Administrative rights on the computer

➤ Completion of Lab 4.1

Estimated completion time: 15 minutes

## Activity Background

Programs can freeze unexpectedly in Windows XP. Whether it's a simple program, such as Notepad, or a complicated program, such as one of the programs in the Office suite, the end result is the same: The program stops and Windows XP tries, by default, to generate an error report to send to Microsoft. In this activity, you get a chance to view the basic contents of an error report.

### ACTIVITY

1. Log on to Test Account #1.

2. Click **Start**, **My Music**, and double-click **Sample Music**. Right-click the New Stories (Highway Blues) icon, click **Open With**, and then click **Notepad**. Click **OK**.

3. Click in the text in the Notepad window, if necessary, press **Ctrl+A**, and then click **Format**, **Font** from the menu.

4. In the Font list box, click **MS Sans Serif**, and in the Font style list box, click **Bold Italic**. In the Size text box, type **72**, and then click **OK**. Click **Format**, **Word Wrap** from the menu.

5. Click **File**, **Save As** from the menu. Click **Desktop** in the Save in list box, and then click **Save**.

6. Immediately and repeatedly click the **Close** button at the top-right corner of the Notepad window. After a few seconds, Notepad stops responding and displays a message box advising you of that fact, as shown in Figure 4-5. Click **End Now**.

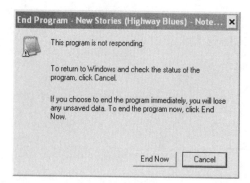

**Figure 4-5**    Program has stopped running

7. In the message box that opens, click the **click here** link. Your screen should resemble Figure 4-6.

8. Read the reporting details, and then click the first **click here** link. Read the technical details in the resulting Error Report Contents message window.

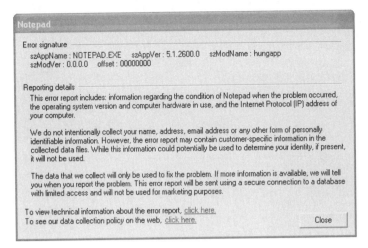

**Figure 4-6**   Error information

9. Click **Close**, click **Close** again, and then click the **Don't Send** button.

10. Log off Test Account #1.

## Certification Objectives

Objectives for Microsoft Exam #70-272: Supporting Users and Troubleshooting Desktop Applications on a Microsoft Windows XP Operating System:

➤ None—Informational only

## Review Questions

1. Notepad can be used to open files other than those with the .txt file extension. True or False?

2. You can access Error Reporting options via the _____ tab of the System Properties dialog box.

3. To send an error report to Microsoft, your computer must have Internet access and encryption capabilities enabled by default. True or False?

4. Which of the following is *not* normally included in the reporting details of an error report in Windows XP?

    a. condition of the program when the problem occurred

    b. the hardware in use

    c. the IP address of your computer

    d. the space left on your hard drive

5. The content of various files on your system can be included with an error report that's sent to Microsoft. True or False?

# 5

# CONFIGURE AND TROUBLESHOOT INTERNET EXPLORER AND OUTLOOK EXPRESS

## Labs included in this chapter:

➤ Lab 5.1 Exploring the Durability of an Internet Explorer Installation

➤ Lab 5.2 Working with Cookies in Internet Explorer

➤ Lab 5.3 Exploring Changes for a Web Content Zone

➤ Lab 5.4 Understanding How Internet Explorer Stores Files

| Microsoft MCDST Exam #70-272 Objectives | |
|---|---|
| Objective | Lab |
| Configure and troubleshoot Internet Explorer. | 5.1, 5.2, 5.3, 5.4 |
| Resolve issues related to Internet Explorer support features. Tasks include configuring Internet Explorer and interpreting error messages. | 5.1, 5.2, 5.3, 5.4 |

## LAB 5.1 EXPLORING THE DURABILITY OF AN INTERNET EXPLORER INSTALLATION

### Objectives

The goal of this lab is to learn first-hand about the durability of Internet Explorer. End users who have used previous versions of Windows operating systems (OSs) might have removed programs at will through Add or Remove Programs or—unacceptably so—through Windows Explorer. However, they won't be able to get away with deleting Internet Explorer in this manner in the latest version of Windows XP. Knowing this durability can help you prioritize your actions when disaster—or perceived disaster—strikes an end user's workstation.

### Materials Required

This lab requires the following:

➤ A computer running Microsoft Windows XP

➤ Administrative rights on the computer

➤ An installation of Internet Explorer with no History (the listing of previously visited sites)

➤ No connection to the Internet

Estimated completion time: 15 minutes

### Activity Background

In this lab, you learn first-hand about the durability of the Internet Explorer installation in the latest version of Windows XP. Knowing about this durability will calm your nerves when you have end users calling and explaining that they were trying to do one thing, but instead they ended up "messing with" or "accidentally deleting" important files for Internet Explorer.

**LAB ACTIVITY**

### ACTIVITY

1. Log on to the computer. You need to log on with administrative rights.

2. Click **Start**, point to **All Programs**, and then click **Internet Explorer**. Note that although Internet Explorer could not load a live page, the program itself still opened, as shown in Figure 5-1.

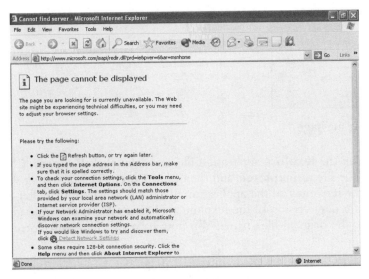

**Figure 5-1**    Internet Explorer window

    3. Open Windows Explorer and navigate to **C:\Program Files\Internet Explorer**. The right side of your screen should resemble Figure 5-2.

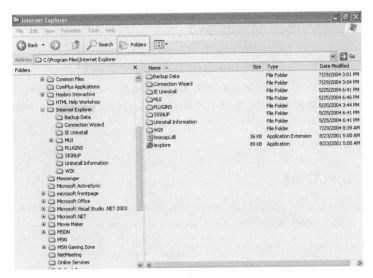

**Figure 5-2**    Internet Explorer files in Windows Explorer

    4. In the right pane, click the **iexplore** application file, and then press the **Delete** key. Click **Yes** in the resulting warning box. After a moment, the image in Figure 5-3 is displayed on your screen. Click **OK**.

**Figure 5-3**   Warning message

5. Right-click the **iexplore** application file, and then click **Rename**. Change the name of the file to **iexploree**, and then press **Enter**. The operating system accepts the renaming of the application file. Note, however, that after a few moments, a new version of the iexplore application file is displayed in the pane and it has the original file's name. You now have two files—iexploree and iexplore.

6. Click **Start**, point to **All Programs**, and then click **Internet Explorer**, if necessary. Note that the application still works as it did at the beginning of this lab.

7. Click **Start**, **Control Panel**, and then double-click **Add or Remove Programs**. Click **Microsoft Internet Explorer 6 SP***x* (*x* is your service pack number), and then click **Change/Remove**. If prompted about additional users on your system, click **Continue**. Note that the options in the resulting message box repair only your installation—they don't remove Internet Explorer functionality for you. If you care to, choose the second option and follow the prompts, restarting your computer when prompted.

8. Log back on to your computer. Click **Start**, point to **All Programs**, and then click **Internet Explorer**. Note that the application still works as it did at the beginning of this lab.

9. Close all open windows.

## Certification Objectives

Objectives for Microsoft Exam #70-272: Supporting Users and Troubleshooting Desktop Applications on a Microsoft Windows XP Operating System:

➤  Configure and troubleshoot Internet Explorer.

➤  Resolve issues related to Internet Explorer support features. Tasks include configuring Internet Explorer and interpreting error messages.

## Review Questions

1. With administrative privileges, you can remove IE from your system. True or False?

2. The Add or Remove Programs feature is accessible through
   _____ .

3. Which of the following is the path to IE files in Windows Explorer?
   a. C:\Windows\Program Files\Internet Explorer
   b. C:\Program Files\Internet Explorer
   c. C:\Inetpub\Internet Explorer
   d. C:\Program Files\System Files\Internet Explorer

4. If necessary, a user with administrative privileges can repair a corrupt installation of IE. True or False?

5. The application file for Internet Explorer can be renamed. True or False?

## Lab 5.2 Working with Cookies in Internet Explorer

### Objectives

The goal of this lab is to familiarize you with cookies, which are small text files containing information about your visits to particular Web sites. The Web site you're visiting *usually* places these files on your computer.

### Materials Required

This lab requires the following:

➤ A computer running Microsoft Windows XP

➤ Administrative rights on the computer

➤ Internet access

➤ A default installation of Internet Explorer

Estimated completion time: 15 minutes

### Activity Background

Cookies—and the related privacy issues—are a concern for many end users and corporations. In this lab, you see first-hand how your actions can permit and deny the placement of cookies on your computer. This knowledge is good to have as end users become more sophisticated in their questions about cookies and privacy.

**ACTIVITY**

1. Log on to the computer. You need to be able to log on with administrative rights.

2. Open Internet Explorer. Click **Tools**, **Internet Options** from the menu. Click the **General** tab, if necessary, and then click the **Delete Cookies** button. Your screen should resemble Figure 5-4. Click **OK**, and then click **OK** again. Leave Internet Explorer open.

**Figure 5-4**    Confirmation message

3. Open Windows Explorer. Expand the elements in the left pane so that you can view **C:\Documents and Settings\\*your account name*\Local Settings\Temporary Internet Files\**. You should see no cookies in this folder, although there might be other files. Leave Windows Explorer open.

**NOTE**
If you can't see the contents of this path, click Tools, Folder Options from the Windows Explorer menu, click the View tab, and then click the Show hidden files and folders option button. Click OK to close the Folder Options dialog box.

4. Return to Internet Explorer. Connect to the Internet and go to **http://finance.yahoo.com**. Click three different links of your choice.

5. Return to your view of Windows Explorer. Press **Ctrl+R** to refresh the screen. Now the Temporary Internet folder contains at least one cookie. (*Note:* You might have to scroll to see this cookie.) Leave Windows Explorer open.

6. Return to Internet Explorer. Click **Tools**, **Internet Options** from the menu. Click the **General** tab, if necessary, and click the **Delete Cookies** button. Click **OK**, and then click **OK** again.

7. Return to Windows Explorer. Press **Ctrl+R** to refresh the screen. Now the Temporary Internet folder contains no cookies. Leave Windows Explorer open.

8. Return to Internet Explorer. Click **Tools**, **Internet Options** from the menu. Click the **Privacy** tab, if necessary. Move the slider on the left up until the identifying text reads "Block All Cookies," as shown in Figure 5-5. Click **OK**.

9. Click three more links at **http://finance.yahoo.com**.

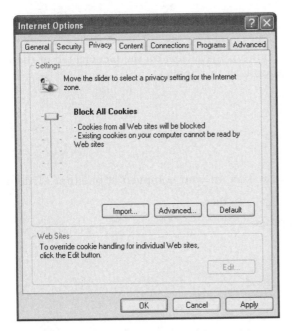

**Figure 5-5**   Blocking cookies

10. Return to Windows Explorer. Press **Ctrl+R** to refresh the screen. The Temporary Internet folder shows no cookies because you blocked their placement.

11. Undo the setting change you made in Step 8.

12. Close Windows Explorer and Internet Explorer, and disconnect from the Internet.

## Certification Objectives

Objectives for Microsoft Exam #70-272: Supporting Users and Troubleshooting Desktop Applications on a Microsoft Windows XP Operating System:

➤ Configure and troubleshoot Internet Explorer.

➤ Resolve issues related to Internet Explorer support features. Tasks include configuring Internet Explorer and interpreting error messages.

## Review Questions

1. You can change cookie settings in the _____ dialog box.

    a. Windows Explorer

    b. Internet Explorer

    c. Internet Options

    d. Control Panel

2. The path to the Temporary Internet Files folder on your computer is
   _____ .

3. Which of the following buttons is available on the General tab of the Internet Options dialog box? (Choose all that apply.)
   a. Clear Settings
   b. User Language
   c. Clear Cookies
   d. Delete Files

4. More than one cookie can exist on your computer at one time. True or False?

5. Cookies are _____ files.
   a. programming language
   b. text
   c. Word
   d. VB. NET

## LAB 5.3 EXPLORING CHANGES FOR A WEB CONTENT ZONE

### Objectives

The goal of this lab is to familiarize you with the concept of Web content zones, which are simply security categories into which you can place Web sites. When Web sites are categorized by content zones, you can set rules for how you want Internet Explorer to interact with those sites. You need to become familiar with zones so that you or other members of your team can help end users deal with the restrictions that might have been placed on Internet Explorer use in your organization.

### Materials Required

This lab requires the following:

➤ A computer running Microsoft Windows XP

➤ Administrative rights on the computer

➤ Default installation of Internet Explorer

➤ Connection to the Internet

Estimated completion time: 15 minutes

## Activity Background

In this lab, you learn about the four Web content zones and how you can change settings for them to meet your organization's security objectives.

**LAB ACTIVITY**

### ACTIVITY

1. Log on to the computer. You need to be able to log on with administrative rights.

2. Open Internet Explorer and connect to the Internet. Go to **www.nbc.com**. Watch the screen to see moving text, flashing text, or pictures that have been switched out for other pictures. These changes happen on your screen because your settings permit the code behind these visuals to operate.

3. Click **Tools**, **Internet Options** from the menu, and then click the **Security** tab. Click the **Internet** icon, if necessary, and then click the **Custom Level** button. Your screen should resemble Figure 5-6.

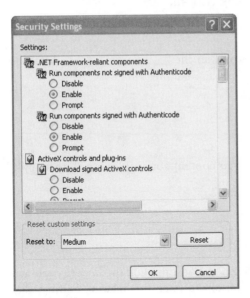

**Figure 5-6**   The Security Settings dialog box

4. In the Settings list box, scroll down to the Run ActiveX controls and plug-ins entry. Click the **Disable** option button, click **OK**, and then click **Yes** to the resulting prompt. Click **OK**. Press **Ctrl+R**. Note the resulting warning about your security settings not permitting the running of ActiveX controls on the page. Click **OK**.

5. Observe the screen and notice that a large section of the graphics at the top of the screen isn't displayed correctly because of the changes in your settings. In essence, you have restricted what the code from this site can do in Internet Explorer on your computer.

6. Undo the setting change you made in Step 4. If time permits, experiment with other settings in the Security Settings dialog box.

7. Disconnect from the Internet, and close Internet Explorer.

## Certification Objectives

Objectives for Microsoft Exam #70-272: Supporting Users and Troubleshooting Desktop Applications on a Microsoft Windows XP Operating System:

➤ Configure and troubleshoot Internet Explorer.

➤ Resolve issues related to Internet Explorer support features. Tasks include configuring Internet Explorer and interpreting error messages.

## Review Questions

1. You can select Web content zones in the _____ dialog box.
   a. Internet Options
   b. Graphics
   c. Security Options
   d. Internet Access

2. Which of the following is a Web content zone? (Choose all that apply.)
   a. Restricted
   b. Trusted sites
   c. Custom
   d. Custom Level

3. In the Internet Options dialog box, you can click the Security tab and then click the _____ button to open the Security Settings dialog box.

4. In the Security Settings dialog box, you can disable more than one option at a time. True or False?

5. You can press _____ to refresh your screen while connected to the Internet.

## LAB 5.4 UNDERSTANDING HOW INTERNET EXPLORER STORES FILES

### Objectives

The goal of this lab is to familiarize you with how IE stores files on your computer; information about this procedure will assist you in helping end users understand why content on their screens change when they revisit a site and why sometimes it does not. This knowledge helps you as a DST because end users will have questions when they use time-sensitive sites with constantly changing content.

### Materials Required

This lab requires the following:

➤ A computer running Microsoft Windows XP

➤ Administrative rights on the computer

➤ Default installation of Internet Explorer

➤ Internet access

Estimated completion time: 15 minutes

### Activity Background

When end users go to sites they have visited before, IE might try to display the site by retrieving previously stored (cached) files on the end user's computer instead of retrieving fresh content (depending on how IE settings have been changed). Retrieving content from the end user's hard drive saves download time. By reconfiguring settings, you can force Internet Explorer to retrieve fresh versions of Web files so that screen content is always timely.

LAB ACTIVITY

### ACTIVITY

1. Log on to the computer. You need to be able to log on with administrative rights.

2. Connect to the Internet, and go to **www.yahoo.com**. Note the time displayed above the In the News tab on the right side.

3. Close Internet Explorer, open it, and return to **www.yahoo.com**. Notice that the time has changed.

4. Click **Tools**, **Internet Options** from the menu, and then click the **Settings** button. Click the **Never** option button, as shown in Figure 5-7, and then click **OK** twice.

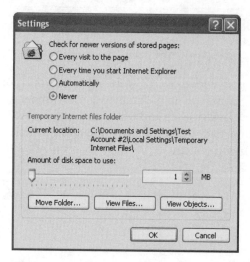

**Figure 5-7** Changing when IE looks for stored pages

5. Close Internet Explorer, wait a few minutes, open it, and return to **www.yahoo.com**. Notice that the time has not changed because the page you're viewing is being loaded from the cache on your computer. That is, the computer was not instructed to look for new content from the Web site, so it didn't.

6. Press **Ctrl+R**, and notice that the time changes.

7. Undo the change you made in Step 4.

8. Disconnect from the Internet, and close all open windows.

## Certification Objectives

Objectives for Microsoft Exam #70-272: Supporting Users and Troubleshooting Desktop Applications on a Microsoft Windows XP Operating System:

➤ Configure and troubleshoot Internet Explorer.

➤ Resolve issues related to Internet Explorer support features. Tasks include configuring Internet Explorer and interpreting error messages.

## Review Questions

1. Which of the following is an option button in the Settings dialog box?

   a. Automatically

   b. Tools

   c. Prompt

   d. On Closing

2. You can change how IE refreshes your screen while you are still connected to the Internet. True or False?

3. The Settings dialog box is accessed through the _____ tab of the Internet Options dialog box.

4. What is the default selection in the Check for newer versions of stored pages: group in the Settings dialog box?

5. If you are signed on to a computer without administrative rights, you can still access the Settings dialog box. True or False?

**5**

# CHAPTER SIX

# INSTALLING OFFICE 2003

---

## Labs included in this chapter:

➤ Lab 6.1 Learning About Your System

➤ Lab 6.2 Understanding the Value of Activation

➤ Lab 6.3 Understanding First Use Among Multiple Users

➤ Lab 6.4 Self-Healing of an Office 2003 Installation Across Users

---

| Microsoft MCDST Exam #70-272 Objectives | |
|---|---|
| Objective | Lab |
| Troubleshoot application installation problems. | 6.1, 6.4 |
| Resolve issues related to Office application support features. Tasks include configuring Office applications and interpreting error messages. | 6.2, 6.3 |
| Personalize Office features. | 6.3 |

## Lab 6.1 Learning About Your System

### Objectives

The goal of this lab is to become proficient in finding information about your system quickly. You—or your end users—need this information to install, reinstall, or make changes to an installation of Office 2003. Without this information, you're only guessing at the system's capability to support Office 2003.

### Materials Required

This lab requires the following:

➤  A computer running Microsoft Windows XP

➤  Administrative rights on the computer

Estimated completion time:  15 minutes

### Activity Background

In this lab, you learn that you can access basic computer information from the command prompt and other locations. Knowing how to access information in this manner should prove useful when you are evaluating equipment in your organization.

LAB ACTIVITY

### Activity

1. Log on to the computer. You need to log on with administrative rights.

2. Click **Start**, point to **All Programs**, point to **Accessories**, and then click **Command Prompt**.

3. Type **cd c:\**, and then press **Enter**. Depending on the size of your Command Prompt window, your screen should resemble Figure 6-1.

4. Type **dir**, and then press **Enter**. Note the number of bytes free in the C: directory on your computer, as shown in the last line of this window. Explore other DOS commands as your instructor recommends.

5. Close the Command Prompt window.

6. Click **Start**, **My Computer**, and then double-click **Local Disk C:\**.

7. Scroll down the left side of your screen, and then click the **Details** double-arrow icon, if necessary. Your screen should resemble Figure 6-2.

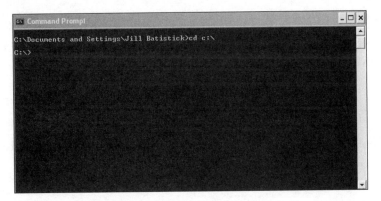

**Figure 6-1** The Command Prompt window

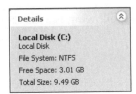

**Figure 6-2** An additional source of system information

8. You can also click **Start**, point to **All Programs**, point to **Accessories**, point to **System Tools**, and then click **System Information**. Depending on your position of the scroll bar on the right side, your screen should resemble Figure 6-3.

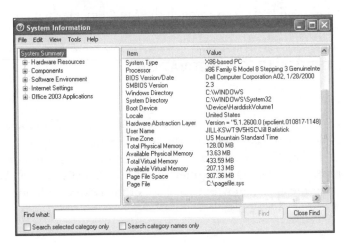

**Figure 6-3** System Information window

9. Close all open windows, and log off.

## Certification Objectives

Objectives for Microsoft Exam #70-272: Supporting Users and Troubleshooting Desktop Applications on a Microsoft Windows XP Operating System:

➤ Troubleshoot application installation problems.

## Review Questions

1. Which of the following is *not* an option available through System Tools?

    a. Activate Windows

    b. System Restore

    c. Disk Cleanup

    d. Command Prompt

2. In the System Information window, which of the following is a category in which summary information is presented?

    a. Windows Directory

    b. OS Manufacturer

    c. Components

    d. OS Name

3. The System Information window contains a search feature. True or False?

4. You can open the Command Prompt window by clicking Start, pointing to All Programs, pointing to _____ , and then clicking Command Prompt.

5. What System Tasks can you access through the My Computer window?

---

# LAB 6.2 UNDERSTANDING THE VALUE OF ACTIVATION

## Objectives

The goal of this lab is to give you an opportunity to see what happens when Office 2003 is not activated within the allowed 50 starts. During the first 50 times you open any Office 2003 application (and the "50 times" is calculated for the applications as a group, not for each application individually), you're prompted to register your Office 2003 software. After the 50th time, you can still open the application, but your use of the features is limited. In this lab, you see the effects of features being disabled.

## Materials Required

This lab requires the following:

➤ A computer running Microsoft Windows XP

➤ Administrative rights on the computer

➤ The installation CDs for Office 2003

Estimated completion time:  30 minutes

## Activity Background

In this lab, you quickly see how frustrating it is to use an application that has been partially disabled because no activation has been performed on an Office 2003 installation.

### ACTIVITY

1. Install Office 2003, but do not activate it.

2. Click **Start**, point to **All Programs**, point to **Microsoft Office**, and then click **Microsoft Office PowerPoint 2003**. You see the first screen of the Activation Wizard.

3. Click **Cancel**, and click the **Close** button in the Task Pane on the right. Your screen should resemble Figure 6-4.

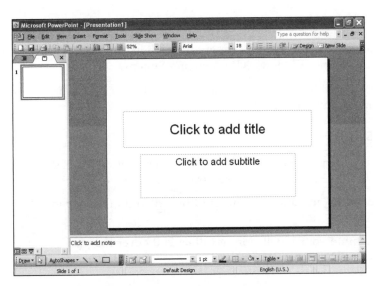

**Figure 6-4**   PowerPoint screen with full features

4. Notice the default toolbars across the top and bottom of the screen. No elements are grayed out (dimmed). If they were, they would be disabled (non-functional).

5. Click the **Click to add title** text in the middle of your screen, type your name, highlight the text, and then press **Ctrl+C**.

6. Click **File** on the menu bar and observe all the available options. Move your mouse to each subsequent menu item to the right of File. Notice all the available options in a fully functional installation of PowerPoint.

7. Save the file by clicking **File**, **Save As** from the menu. Accept the default name and the default folder, and then click **Save**. Close PowerPoint.

8. Now's the time to refresh your coffee because you are going to open and close that same file 50 times or until you pass the activation threshold limit set by Microsoft.

9. Open your file after the grace number of times permitted for your installation of Office 2003. Notice the dimmed toolbars at the top and bottom of the screen.

10. Explore the menu options. Notice that most of the previous options are no longer available.

11. Close all open windows.

12. Activate your installation of Office 2003, if your instructor tells you to do so.

13. Log off.

## Certification Objectives

Objectives for Microsoft Exam #70-272: Supporting Users and Troubleshooting Desktop Applications on a Microsoft Windows XP Operating System:

➤ Resolve issues related to Office application support features. Tasks include configuring Office applications and interpreting error messages.

## Review Questions

1. When you start a default installation of PowerPoint or Word, the Task Pane opens on the left side of the screen by default. True or False?

2. What does the activation feature of Office 2003 do for your installation of Office 2003?

3. If you activate your installation of Office 2003 over the phone, you supply an installation ID and receive a(n) _____ ID.

4. An installation ID is an alphanumeric string of characters that you look up through System Properties. True or False?

5. You must activate Office 2003 each time you install one of its applications. True or False?

---

## LAB 6.3 UNDERSTANDING FIRST USE AMONG MULTIPLE USERS

### Objectives

The goal of this lab is to show you that each user on your computer must install Office 2003 applications for his or her use when those applications are installed with the On First Use feature. Note that these installations pick up custom information from each user's profile. This feature should make your end users happy because they don't have to reenter or reestablish much of the information in their profiles.

### Materials Required

This lab requires the following:

➤ A computer running Microsoft Windows XP

➤ Administrative rights on the computer

➤ Default installation of Office 2003

Estimated completion time:  15 minutes

### Activity Background

In this lab, you find that even if users have to install their applications individually, their language preferences (a representative feature of customization) carry over into their installation. Knowing this fact can make life easier for you if, during deployment, users come to you concerned that their carefully set options won't carry over into their new work environment.

LAB ACTIVITY

### ACTIVITY

1. Create two new user accounts. Name the first one **Activation One** and give it administrative privileges by clicking the **Computer administrator** option button. Name the second one **Activation Two** and give it administrative privileges as well.

2. Log on as **Activation One**. Click **Start**, if necessary, and then click **Control Panel**. If necessary, click **Switch to Classic View**. Double-click **Regional and Language Options**, click the **Regional Options** tab, click the **Standards and formats** list arrow, and then click **German (Germany)**. Click **OK**, and then close Control Panel.

3. Click **Start**, point to **All Programs**, point to **Microsoft Office**, and then click **Microsoft Office Word 2003**. Notice the Installation progress message box on the screen.

4. Word 2003 opens. Click **OK** to the User Name dialog box prompt.

5. Click **Tools** on the menu bar, point to **Language**, and then click **Set Language**. Notice that German (Germany) is listed, along with English, at the top of the Language dialog box, as shown in Figure 6-5.

**Figure 6-5**    Language preference for the Activation One account

6. Click **Cancel** and then close Word. If necessary, click **No** to any additional prompts.

7. Log off as Activation One and log on as **Activation Two**.

8. Repeat Step 2 for the Activation Two account, but make your language choice **Uzbek (Cyrillic)**.

9. Repeat Steps 3 and 4. When you try to open Word, notice that you see the same Installation progress message box you did when you were using the Activation One account in Step 3.

10. Repeat Step 5, but notice the different language setup. It reflects Uzbek (Cyrillic), as shown in Figure 6-6. Word was installed in a custom manner for this user as well.

11. Close Word and do not save your changes.

12. Log off.

**Figure 6-6**   Language preference for the Activation Two account

## Certification Objectives

Objectives for Microsoft Exam #70-272: Supporting Users and Troubleshooting Desktop Applications on a Microsoft Windows XP Operating System:

➤ Resolve issues related to Office application support features. Tasks include configuring Office applications and interpreting error messages.

➤ Personalize Office features.

## Review Questions

1. The On First Use feature works only with accounts that have administrative privileges. True or False?

2. In the Regional and Language Options applet, for what four elements can you customize settings?

3. Which of the following is a tab in the Regional and Language Options dialog box?

   a. Long Date

   b. Standards and Formats

   c. Advanced

   d. Preferences

4. A default installation of Windows XP gives you the option of supporting right-to-left languages in Word. True or False?

5. You can access the Regional and Language Options applet through _____ .

## LAB 6.4 SELF-HEALING OF AN OFFICE 2003 INSTALLATION ACROSS USERS

### Objectives

As an end user, your installation of Office 2003 will be available to other users of your computer. At times, users' actions can cause the installation to become corrupt. Fortunately, Office 2003 repairs itself—under most conditions—and the repairs hold across different user environments.

### Materials Required

This lab requires the following:

➤ A computer running Microsoft Windows XP

➤ Administrative rights on the computer

➤ A default installation of Office 2003

➤ Completion of Lab 6.3

Estimated completion time:  15 minutes

### Activity Background

In this lab, you learn that Office 2003 can fix itself if end users meddle with your installation of this application. Knowing this can make you a calmer DST because you'll know what user actions can result in you working late to repair problems and what actions have no effect on whether you can go home on time.

LAB ACTIVITY

### ACTIVITY

1. Log on to the computer with the **Activation One** account.

2. Right-click **Start**, click **Explore**, and navigate to **C:\Program Files\Microsoft Office**. Right-click **Microsoft Office**, and then click **Properties**. Click to clear the **Read-only** check box, and then click **OK**. Your screen should resemble Figure 6-7. Click **OK**.

3. Try to delete the folder. Note that your action has no permanent effect. Click **OK**. Right-click **Start**, click **Explore**, and navigate to **C:\Program Files\Microsoft Office**, if necessary. Right-click **Microsoft Office**, and then click **Properties**. Notice that the Read-only setting is still enabled. Click **Cancel**.

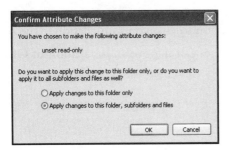

**Figure 6-7**    The Confirm Attribute Changes dialog box

6

4. Log off as Activation One and log on as **Activation Two**. Right-click **Start**, click **Explore**, and navigate to **C:\Program Files\Microsoft Office\OFFICE11**. In the right pane, right-click the **POWERPNT** file, and then click **Properties**. Note that this file is not a read-only file. Click **OK**, and then press the **Delete** key. Click **Yes** to the resulting prompt.

5. Log off as Activation Two, and log on as **Activation One**. Click **Start**, point to **All Programs**, point to **Microsoft Office**, and then click **Microsoft Office PowerPoint 2003**. The program is installed for the Activation One account, in spite of the actions you performed under the Activation Two account. (Note that you might be prompted for the installation CD during this step.)

6. Close all open windows, and log off.

## Certification Objectives

Objectives for Microsoft Exam #70-272: Supporting Users and Troubleshooting Desktop Applications on a Microsoft Windows XP Operating System:

➤ Troubleshoot application installation problems.

## Review Questions

1. In a normal installation of Office 2003, you cannot delete the Microsoft Office folder from Explorer. True or False?

2. In an installation of Office 2003 that has not been activated, you can delete the Microsoft Office folder from Explorer. True or False?

3. An installation of Office 2003 that has passed its 50-usage limit and now needs to be activated still appears in the Add or Remove Programs window. True or False?

4. If an element appears in the Add or Remove Programs window, you always have the Change button as an option to change its installation. True or False?

5. A user with administrative privileges can remove an installation of Office 2003 from a workstation. True or False?

# 7

# CONFIGURING AND TROUBLESHOOTING OPERATING SYSTEM FEATURES

## Labs included in this chapter:

➤ Lab 7.1 Finding Lost Files

➤ Lab 7.2 Backing up a Team's Files

➤ Lab 7.3 Using the Add Scheduled Task Feature

➤ Lab 7.4 Understanding Performance Options

| Microsoft MCDST Exam #70-272 Objectives | |
|---|---|
| Objective | Lab |
| Resolve issues related to operating system features. Tasks include configuring operating system features and interpreting error messages. | 7.1, 7.2, 7.3, 7.4 |
| Answer end-user questions related to customizing the operating system to support an application. | 7.3, 7.4 |

## LAB 7.1 FINDING LOST FILES

### Objectives

The goal of this lab is to become proficient in finding "lost" files. The term "lost" is used loosely because when an end user tells you he or she has "lost" a file, it's rarely "lost" as in "irretrievable." It's usually "lost" as in "I don't remember where I put it." Although you often find these lost files in the Documents and Settings\\*user name* folder, you might have to hunt for others.

### Materials Required

This lab requires the following:

➤  A computer running Microsoft Windows XP

➤  Administrative rights on the computer

➤  A partner

Estimated completion time: 15 minutes

### Activity Background

In this lab, you know that most files are automatically saved to the My Documents folder of the user account on which the activity was performed. Sometimes, however, end users place the files elsewhere—sometimes by accident and sometimes by design. Knowing how to do even a rudimentary search can save you and your end users plenty of time and aggravation.

LAB ACTIVITY

### ACTIVITY

1.  Log on to the computer. You need to log on with administrative rights. Ask your partner to look away while you perform Steps 2 through 4.

2.  Click **Start**, point to **All Programs**, point to **Accessories**, and then click **Notepad**.

3.  Type your name and the date in the body of the document. Click **File**, **Save As** from the menu.

4.  Click the **Save in** list arrow, select a folder where you wouldn't normally place your file (but don't save it to the desktop—that's too easy). Remember that you're trying to "hide" this file from your partner. In the File name text box, give the file a name that you won't share with your partner, and then click **Save**. Close Notepad.

5. Give control of the computer over to your partner. Your partner will perform the remaining steps. (Note that the format of the steps stays the same for brevity.)

6. Right-click **Start**, and then click **Explore**. Click the **Search** button on the Standard toolbar. Your screen should resemble Figure 7-1.

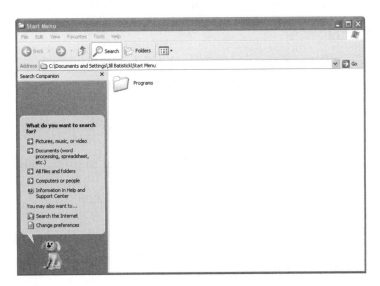

**Figure 7-1** Performing a search

7. Click **All file and folders**. Click the **When was it modified?** arrow button. Click the **Specify dates** option button, click **Created Date** in the accompanying list box, and then set the from and to list boxes to today's date (if necessary).

8. Click **Search**. Did your search produce your partner's file? If not, click the **Back** button in the Search Companion. Notice that the Look in list box has "Start Menu" by default. Click the accompanying list arrow and note that you see a hierarchy similar to that seen in Windows Explorer. Click **My Computer**, and then click **Search**.

9. Click the headers at the top of the Search Results window, as shown in Figure 7-2, to change the sorting of the files until you spot the one you're looking for. Close the Search Results window, and log off.

**Figure 7-2** Use the headers to sort your search

## Certification Objectives

Objectives for Microsoft Exam #70-272: Supporting Users and Troubleshooting Desktop Applications on a Microsoft Windows XP Operating System:

➤ Resolve issues related to operating system features. Tasks include configuring operating system features and interpreting error messages.

## Review Questions

1. Under what folder are user folders located in Windows Explorer?

2. A user-created folder can be selected in the Look in list box of the Search Companion. True or False?

3. What are some of the date-based options in the Windows XP Search Companion?

4. The animated character in the Search Companion can be turned off to suit your end user's preference. True or False?

5. The Search option in Windows XP can be accessed only through the Start Menu window. True or False?

## LAB 7.2 BACKING UP A TEAM'S FILES

### Objectives

The goal of this lab is to learn that you can back up multiple end users' work to one folder. This feature can be useful for the supervisors in your organization. Each supervisor can have the work of his or her team backed up regularly to one location for safekeeping. That way, should there be a problem with one team's workstation(s), the location of all the team's work is in one easily recoverable location.

### Materials Required

This lab requires the following:

➤ A computer running Microsoft Windows XP

➤ An account with administrative rights on the computer

➤ Completion of Lab 6.3

Estimated completion time: 15 minutes

## Activity Background

In this lab, you find out how easy it is to back up end-user folders for use in your organization. Knowing how to do this allows you to provide good and effective customer service to your end users.

### ACTIVITY

1. Log on as **Activation One**. Right-click **Start**, click **Explore**, and then expand the folders to **Local Disk (C:)\Documents and Settings\Activation One**. Click the **Activation One** folder, click **File** on the menu bar, point to **New**, and then click **Folder**. Type **Activation One Backup Test** and then press **Enter**.

2. Click **Start**, point to **All Programs**, point to **Accessories**, and then click **Notepad**. Type **Activation One Backup Test**. Click **File, Save As** from the menu, click the **Save In** list box arrow, and click **Local Disk (C:)**. Double-click **Documents and Settings**, double-click **Activation One**, and double-click **Activation One Backup Test**. Type **Activation One** in the File name list box, click **Save**, and then close Notepad.

3. Log off as Activation One, and log on as **Activation Two**. Repeat Steps 1 and 2 for the Activation Two account, substituting the name accordingly. Log off the Activation Two account.

4. Log on with your own administrator account. Right-click **Start**, click **Explore**, and then click **Local Disk (C:)**. Click **File** on the menu bar, point to **New**, and then click **Folder**. Name the folder **A Weekly Folder**. (The name was chosen to make it show up close to the top of the hierarchy of folders.)

5. To start the Backup or Restore Wizard, click **Start**, point to **All Programs**, point to **Accessories**, point to **System Tools**, and then click **Backup**. Click **Next** twice, which brings you to the screen shown in Figure 7-3.

6. Click the **Let me choose what to back up** option button, and then click **Next**.

7. In the Items to back up pane on the left, navigate to and click to select the check boxes to the left of the **Activation One Backup Test** and **Activation Two Backup Test** folders. Click **Next**. In the Choose a place to save your backup list box, click the **Browse** button. Navigate to **C:\A Weekly Folder**, and then click **Save**. Click **Next**, and then click **Finish**. While you wait for the backup to finish, your screen will resemble Figure 7-4.

8. When the backup is finished, click **Close**.

9. Open Windows Explorer, if it is not already open. Navigate to **Local Disk (C:)\A Weekly Folder**. In this folder is Backup, which is a Windows Backup File.

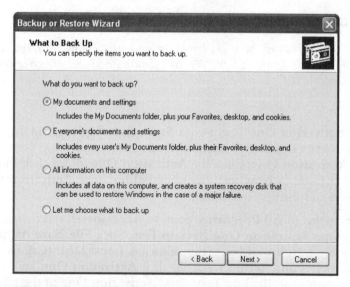

**Figure 7-3**   Specifying what you want to back up

**Figure 7-4**   Backup progress

10. Right-click the file, and then click **Open With**. Click **Windows Backup Utility**, if necessary, and then click **OK**. This brings you back to the Backup or Restore Wizard window, where you can perform the backup restore.

11. Click **Cancel** because you are not going to perform the restore at this time.

12. Close all open windows, and log off.

## Certification Objectives

Objectives for Microsoft Exam #70-272: Supporting Users and Troubleshooting Desktop Applications on a Microsoft Windows XP Operating System:

➤ Resolve issues related to operating system features. Tasks include configuring operating system features and interpreting error messages.

## Review Questions

1. To open the Backup utility, click Start, point to All Programs, point to Accessories, point to _____ , and then click Backup.

2. You can back up files that you did not create. True or False?

3. What are the four options in the What to Back Up screen of the Backup or Restore Wizard?

4. If you click the Let me choose what to back up option button in the Backup or Restore Wizard, you can still select the contents of the My Documents folder to be backed up, even though this option is also listed under the My documents and settings option in the same wizard. True or False?

5. In the Backup Progress dialog box, you can learn how many files the wizard has processed, but not the disk drive involved. True or False?

7

---

# LAB 7.3 USING THE ADD SCHEDULED TASK FEATURE

## Objectives

The goal of this lab is to show you how to schedule different events on an end user's computer. When you show end users how to use this feature, they find that tasks that are easily forgotten can be made to pop up automatically in reminders.

## Materials Required

This lab requires the following:

➤ A computer running Microsoft Windows XP

➤ Administrative rights on the computer that has a password

➤ Microsoft Office 2003

➤ No other users logged on to your computer

Estimated completion time: 15 minutes

## Activity Background

In this lab, you see how you can have an event occur because of something a user has done—logged on—or because the system has reached a certain time on its clock. Either way, after your users know how to use this feature, they will find that it adds efficiency to their workdays.

**LAB ACTIVITY**

## ACTIVITY

1. Log on to the computer. You need to log on with administrative rights.

2. Click **Start**, point to **All Programs**, point to **Accessories**, point to **System Tools**, and then click **Scheduled Tasks**. Double-click **Add Scheduled Task** to open the wizard, shown in Figure 7-5, and then click **Next**.

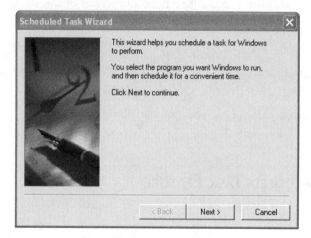

**Figure 7-5**   The Scheduled Task Wizard

3. Click **Microsoft Office Word 2003** in the Application list (you might have to scroll to see the selection), and then click **Next**.

4. Click the **When I log on** option button, click **Next**, enter your user name, enter the password for your account, and then click **Next**. Click **Finish**. Close the Scheduled Tasks window.

5. Log off your account and restart your computer. Log back on. Microsoft Office Word 2003 should open automatically. Close Word.

**NOTE**

If other users are currently logged on to your computer, the automatic startup might not happen.

6. You can also set actions to occur at a specific time. Repeat Step 2 to open the Scheduled Task Wizard again. Click **Next**. Click **Freecell** in the Application list, and then click **Next**. Click the **Daily** option button, and then click **Next**. Set the Start time to a few minutes ahead of the current time. Click **Next**, and enter the password information. Click **Next**.

7. Click **Finish**. The Freecell application will open on the schedule you set.

**NOTE**    Users like to use the timed option to set fun games at closing time. There's nothing like a cheerful game popping up on your screen to let you know that it's time to go home.

7

8. Close all open windows, and log off.

## Certification Objectives

Objectives for Microsoft Exam #70-272: Supporting Users and Troubleshooting Desktop Applications on a Microsoft Windows XP Operating System:

➤ Resolve issues related to operating system features. Tasks include configuring operating system features and interpreting error messages.

➤ Answer end-user questions related to customizing the operating system to support an application.

## Review Questions

1. After you set a scheduled task, it's listed in the Scheduled Tasks window until you delete it. True or False?

2. In the screen in which you select applications for the Scheduled Task Wizard, you can see a list of applications and _____ information about those applications.

3. The applications listed in the Scheduled Task Wizard are identical from computer to computer. True or False.

4. List three time frames in which you can set scheduled tasks in the Scheduled Task Wizard.

5. You can set an event in the Scheduled Task Wizard to be a one-time event. True or False?

## Lab 7.4 Understanding Performance Options

### Objectives

The goal of this lab is to familiarize you with the different settings in the Performance Options dialog box. Whether you are helping users make changes they need—such as having content visible in dragged windows—or changes they want—such as the appearance of icons on the screen—you'll be a more valuable DST if you can answer questions quickly and efficiently.

### Materials Required

This lab requires the following:

➤ A computer running Microsoft Windows XP

➤ Administrative rights on the computer

Estimated completion time: 15 minutes

### Activity Background

In this lab, you discover that options in the Performance Options dialog box have somewhat low-key effects on the system. Nonetheless, users often want these options in their work environment. Unless you are violating company policy for user desktops, it's your job to help users learn how to make these changes.

LAB ACTIVITY

### Activity

1. Log on to the computer. You need to log on with administrative rights.

2. Click **Start**, right-click **My Computer**, and then click **Properties**. In the System Properties dialog box, click the **Advanced** tab, and then click the **Settings** button in the Performance section. Click the **Visual Effects** tab, if necessary. Your screen should resemble Figure 7-6.

3. Move the Performance Options dialog box so that you can see at least one icon on your desktop. Click the **Custom** option button, if necessary. Click to clear the **Use drop shadows for icon labels on the desktop** check box, watch the icon(s) on your desktop, and then click **Apply**. Notice the change in the icon label(s) on your desktop.

4. Leave the dialog box on your screen, but open the Notepad and Paint applications and then minimize them so that they appear as buttons on your taskbar. Notice the style of the buttons. In the Performance Options dialog box, scroll down the list box, click to clear the **Use visual styles on windows and buttons** check box, and then click **Apply**. Notice the difference in the presentation of the buttons on your taskbar.

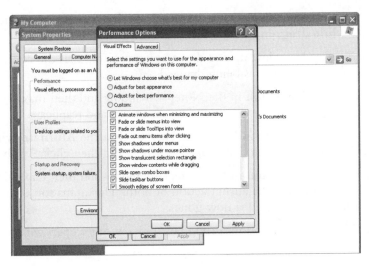

**Figure 7-6**   Setting performance options

5.  Maximize the Notepad application. Resize the window so that it takes up about a quarter of the screen, as shown in Figure 7-7.

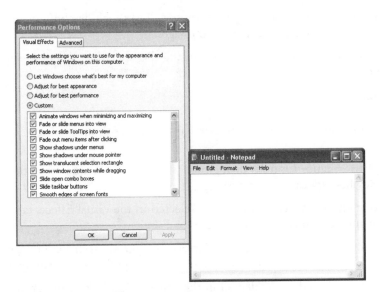

**Figure 7-7**   Placement of Notepad window

6.  Type your name in the window. Drag the window up and down, noticing how you can still see the content of the window as you drag it.

7. In the Performance Options dialog box, click to clear the **Show window contents while dragging** check box, and then click **Apply**.

8. Drag the Notepad window up and down again, noticing that the content disappears while the window is being dragged.

9. Click the **Minimize** button in the Notepad window and then maximize the window again, noticing how the window disappears and reappears.

10. In the Performance Options dialog box, click to clear the **Animate windows when minimizing or maximizing** check box, and then click **Apply**.

11. Click the **Minimize** button in the Notepad window and then maximize the window again, noticing the abrupt action of both. The animation that caused the smooth action of Step 9 is now gone.

12. Close the Performance Options dialog box and any other open windows, and log off.

## Certification Objectives

Objectives for Microsoft Exam #70-272: Supporting Users and Troubleshooting Desktop Applications on a Microsoft Windows XP Operating System:

➤ Resolve issues related to operating system features. Tasks include configuring operating system features and interpreting error messages.

➤ Answer end-user questions related to customizing the operating system to support an application.

## Review Questions

1. The Performance Options dialog box has two tabs: Advanced and
   _____ .

2. In the Performance Options dialog box, you can have Windows set the adjustments for best appearance or best _____ .

3. Only one check box at a time can be selected in the Visual Effects tab of the Performance Options dialog box. True or False?

4. The effects of choices made in the Performance Options dialog box can show up in both Office applications and system utility applications. True or False?

5. For options selected or deselected in the Visual Effects tab of the Performance Options dialog box to have an effect, you must restart your computer. True or False?

# RESOLVING ISSUES RELATED TO OFFICE APPLICATION USAGE

## Labs included in this chapter:

➤ Lab 8.1 Working with Toolbars and Menus
➤ Lab 8.2 Exploring the Options Dialog Box
➤ Lab 8.3 Using AutoCorrect
➤ Lab 8.4 Using Microsoft Office Picture Manager

| Microsoft MCDST Exam #70-272 Objectives | |
|---|---|
| Objective | Lab |
| Set application compatibility settings. | 8.2 |
| Answer end-user questions related to customizing Office applications. | 8.1, 8.2, 8.3 |
| Customize toolbars. | 8.1 |
| Personalize Office features. | 8.1, 8.2, 8.3 |

## LAB 8.1 WORKING WITH TOOLBARS AND MENUS

### Objectives

The goal of this lab is to make you solidly proficient in manipulating toolbars and menus within the Office 2003 environment. Although this skill set doesn't get the accolades of some of its more sophisticated brethren—such as knowing how to manipulate photos or send broadcast e-mails—it's a skill set that comes into use every day, in every application, and in every file.

### Materials Required

This lab requires the following:

➤ A computer running Microsoft Windows XP

➤ Administrative rights on the computer

➤ A default installation of Microsoft Office 2003

Estimated completion time: 15 minutes

### Activity Background

In this lab, you discover that manipulating toolbars and menus appeals to most end users. The more they can customize their work environment, the more confident they feel with the technology on their computers. And the more comfortable they feel, the less they need to rely on you.

**LAB ACTIVITY**

### ACTIVITY

1. Log on to the computer. You need to log on with administrative rights.

2. Click **Start**, point to **All Programs**, point to **Microsoft Office**, and then click **Microsoft Office PowerPoint 2003**.

3. Close the Task Pane, if necessary.

4. Right-click any toolbar in the screen to bring up the list of available toolbars, as shown in Figure 8-1.

5. Click to clear the **Standard** toolbar entry in the list, and notice that the toolbar is removed from the PowerPoint window. Repeat Step 4, and then click to enable the **Standard** entry again. Notice that the toolbar is restored.

6. Repeat Steps 4 and 5 for the Formatting and Drawing toolbars.

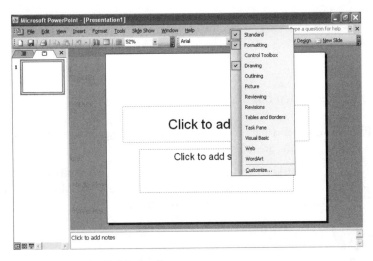

**Figure 8-1**   Available toolbars

7. Right-click a toolbar, and then click the **Tables and Borders** entry. Notice that the toolbar appears in the middle of your work area, as shown in Figure 8-2.

**Figure 8-2**   Tables and Borders toolbar

8. Click and hold the title bar of the Tables and Borders toolbar. Notice that your mouse cursor turns into a four-headed arrow. Drag the toolbar to the bottom of your screen until it's docked above (stacked on top of) the Drawing toolbar, but don't let go of the mouse button.

9. Continue dragging the toolbar down until it's placed on the same row as the Drawing toolbar, as shown in Figure 8-3, and then release the mouse button.

Toolbar Options list arrow

**Figure 8-3**   Two toolbars on one row

10. Notice that you can't see as many buttons on the Drawing toolbar in Figure 8-3 as you could see in Figure 8-1. Click the **Toolbar Options** list arrow on the Drawing toolbar to see the missing buttons, shown in Figure 8-4.

8

**Figure 8-4**   Displaying the hidden buttons

11. Click **File** on the menu bar, and observe the ordering of the first three menu options. Those options are New, Open, and Close.

12. Click **Tools**, **Customize** from the menu, click the **Commands** tab, and then click the **Rearrange Commands** button. Your screen should resemble Figure 8-5 if you have a default installation of Office 2003.

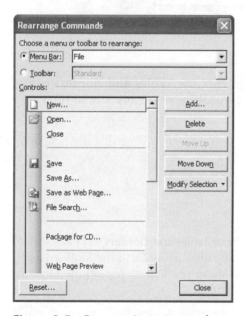

**Figure 8-5**   Rearranging commands

13. Click the **Move Down** button, and notice that the New menu option is now below the Open menu option.

14. Click the **Modify Selection** button, and change the Name entry to **&Testing....** Press **Enter**. Click **Close**, and click **Close** again.

15. Click **File** on the menu bar, and notice the new entry in the second position.

16. Undo the changes you made in Steps 13 and 14.

17. Exit PowerPoint, and log off.

## Certification Objectives

Objectives for Microsoft Exam #70-272: Supporting Users and Troubleshooting Desktop Applications on a Microsoft Windows XP Operating System:

➤ Answer end-user questions related to customizing Office applications.

➤ Customize toolbars.

➤ Personalize Office features.

## Review Questions

1. List and describe three common toolbars in an Office application.

2. The three tabs in the Customize dialog box are Options, Toolbars, and

   _____ .

3. What tasks can you accomplish with the Rearrange Commands dialog box?

4. From the Rearrange Commands dialog box, you can rename a menu item in the Controls list by clicking the _____ button and then changing the name in the appropriate location.

5. Items in the Controls list in the Rearrange Commands dialog box can be dragged to change their order. True or False?

8

## LAB 8.2 EXPLORING THE OPTIONS DIALOG BOX

### Objectives

The goal of this lab is to become familiar with the myriad of options in the Options dialog box of an Office application. Although the content of this dialog box can differ from application to application, the basic premise is the same: You use the options to change how your software displays, saves, secures, and generally manipulates your work.

### Materials Required

This lab requires the following:

➤ A computer running Microsoft Windows XP

➤ Administrative rights on the computer

➤ A default installation of Microsoft Office 2003

Estimated completion time: 15 minutes

## Activity Background

In this lab, you discover that the Options dialog box contains options that end users often want to use. They might not know how to get to these options but have likely seen the options in effect on other users' workstations. Be sure you know these options thoroughly so that when an end user describes them, you know exactly what he or she is trying to reference.

## ACTIVITY

1. Log on to the computer. You need to log on with administrative rights.

2. Click **Start**, point to **All Programs**, point to **Microsoft Office**, and then click **Microsoft Office PowerPoint 2003**.

3. Close the Task Pane, if necessary.

4. Press **Ctrl+S**. Accept the default Save in location, type **Test 1** in the File name text box, and press **Enter**.

5. Press **Ctrl+N** to open a new presentation.

6. Press **Ctrl+S**. Accept the default Save in location, type **Test 2** in the File name text box, and press **Enter**.

7. Look at the taskbar on your screen. Both PowerPoint presentations are present on the taskbar, each displaying its own name, as shown in Figure 8-6.

**Figure 8-6**　PowerPoint presentations on the taskbar

8. Click **Tools, Options** from the menu. Click the **View** tab, if necessary, and then click to clear the **Windows in Taskbar** check box. Click **OK**. Notice that the Test 1 and Test 2 windows have been removed from the taskbar.

9. Undo the change you made in Step 8, and with the Options dialog box still open, click the **Security** tab.

10. In the Password to open text box, type **MyPassword**. Click **OK**, and then reenter the password when prompted. Click **OK**.

11. Close the Test 2 file, and click **Yes** when prompted to save the changes.

12. Click **File** on the menu bar, and then click **Test 2**. You should see a Password dialog box similar to the one in Figure 8-7.

13. Type **MyPassword**, and then click **OK** to open the file.

14. Close the file and exit PowerPoint.

15. Log off.

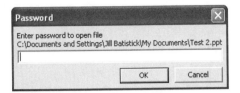

**Figure 8-7**    Password dialog box

## Certification Objectives

Objectives for Microsoft Exam #70-272: Supporting Users and Troubleshooting Desktop Applications on a Microsoft Windows XP Operating System:

➤ Set application compatibility settings.

➤ Answer end-user questions related to customizing Office applications.

➤ Personalize Office features.

## Review Questions

1. Describe two tasks you can accomplish in the Security tab of the Options dialog box.

2. By default, the Save AutoRecover info every option in the Save tab of the dialog box is set to _____ minutes.

3. In PowerPoint, the default save location for a file is C:\Documents and Settings\*your user name*\My Documents\. True or False?

4. In the Edit tab of the Options dialog box, the Maximum number of undos option can be set to a double-digit number. True or False?

5. Name at least two options in the Spelling and Style tab of the Options dialog box.

## LAB 8.3 USING AUTOCORRECT

### Objectives

The goal of this lab is to become proficient in the tools housed under the AutoCorrect tab of the AutoCorrect dialog box in Microsoft Office Word 2003. Admittedly, the options are simple, but mastering them and teaching your end users how to use them can take the drudgery out of highly repetitive tasks. The more drudgery you can avoid, the more energy you'll have for the tasks that make your career shine.

## Materials Required

This lab requires the following:

➤ A computer running Microsoft Windows XP

➤ Administrative rights on the computer

➤ A default installation of Microsoft Office 2003

Estimated completion time: 15 minutes

## Activity Background

In this lab, you explore the AutoCorrect tab. When you are comfortable with these options, you should have no trouble exploring the other tabs—AutoText, AutoFormat, and so on—in the AutoCorrect dialog box and showing your end users how to carve a bit more time out of their busy workdays.

LAB ACTIVITY

### ACTIVITY

1. Log on to the computer. You need to log on with administrative rights.

2. Click **Start**, point to **All Programs**, point to **Microsoft Office**, and then click **Microsoft Office Word 2003**.

3. Close the Task Pane, if necessary.

4. Type your name on the screen, but do not press **Enter**.

5. Click **Tools**, **AutoCorrect Options** from the menu. If necessary, click the **AutoCorrect** tab.

6. In the Replace text box, type your name.

7. In the With text box, type **I am the best student in the class.**.

8. Click **Add**, and notice that the new entry is added to the list box below the text boxes, as shown in Figure 8-8. Click **OK**.

9. Press the **Enter** key. Your name changes to the new text. Type your name again, and then press the **spacebar**. The text appears again. Press **Enter**.

10. Type **youve**, and then press the **spacebar**. Notice that Word has changed your entered text to "You've." Press **Enter**.

11. Click **Tools**, **AutoCorrect Options** from the menu. Click the **AutoCorrect** tab, if necessary.

12. In the list box at the bottom of the tab, scroll down and select the **youve** option. Click the **Delete** button. Notice that Word moves the youve entry to the Replace text box above. Click the **Add** button. Notice that Word moves the youve entry back to the list box at the bottom of the tab.

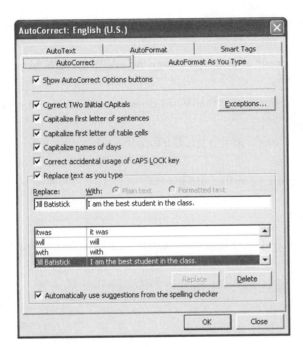

**Figure 8-8**   Using AutoCorrect

13. In the With text box, type **You've got a friend.**, and then click **Replace**. Click **Yes** to the prompt, as shown in Figure 8-9. Click **OK**.

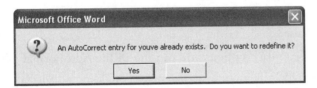

**Figure 8-9**   Replacement prompt

14. Type **youve** and then press the **spacebar**. Pretty cool, no?

15. Press the **Caps Lock** key on your keyboard. Above the keypad on your keyboard, you might see a small light next to the words "Caps Lock" to indicate that Caps Lock is on. Press the **Shift** key, and type **T**. Look at the screen. The letter came out as a lowercase letter because pressing the Shift key while the Caps Lock key is on negates the Caps Lock effect.

16. Let go of the Shift key, and then type **H**. Your screen should have the text "tH." Type **IS**. Your screen should now have this text: "tHIS."

17. Press **Enter**. Word corrects your text to "This."

18. Press the **Caps Lock** key on your keyboard to toggle the feature off.

19. Click **Tools, AutoCorrect Options**. Click the **AutoCorrect** tab, if necessary.

20. Click to clear the **Correct accidental usage of cAPS LOCK key** check box, and then click **OK**.

21. Repeat Steps 15 to 17, but notice that Word doesn't make the same correction in Step 17 that it did before.

22. Undo the changes you made in this lab. Explore the other tabs, as time permits.

23. Exit Word without saving your file, and log off.

## Certification Objectives

Objectives for Microsoft Exam #70-272: Supporting Users and Troubleshooting Desktop Applications on a Microsoft Windows XP Operating System:

➤ Answer end-user questions related to customizing Office applications.

➤ Personalize Office features.

## Review Questions

1. What can you do with the Exceptions button in the AutoCorrect tab of the AutoCorrect dialog box?

2. Discuss at least three options you can access in the AutoFormat As You Type tab of the AutoCorrect dialog box.

3. You can apply a smart tag to a numerical piece of text, such as a telephone number. True or False?

4. Discuss at least three replace options you can use in the AutoFormat tab of the AutoCorrect dialog box.

5. In the AutoFormat tab of the AutoCorrect dialog box, you can preserve the styles of changed text. True or False?

## Lab 8.4 Using Microsoft Office Picture Manager

### Objectives

The goal of this lab is to familiarize you with the Microsoft Office Picture Manager. As your end users acquire more pictures—whether from cameras, the latest cell phones, or the Internet—they will appreciate one piece of software that can be used for basic organizing and manipulating. Microsoft Office Picture Manager is no Photoshop, but it performs many of the common tasks that end users often need.

## Materials Required

This lab requires the following:

➤ A computer running Microsoft Windows XP

➤ Administrative rights on the computer

➤ A default installation of Microsoft Office 2003

Estimated completion time: 15 minutes

**8**

## Activity Background

In this lab, you learn that Microsoft Office Picture Manager is relatively simple to use. Whether your end users need help with cropping a favorite work photo or simply want to touch up a photo before it heads to the company intranet, they will find this software to be a convenient addition to the Microsoft Office 2003 suite.

**LAB ACTIVITY**

### ACTIVITY

1. Log on to the computer. You need to log on with administrative rights.

2. Open Windows Explorer, and click **Local Disk (C:)**. Click **File** on the menu bar, point to **New**, and then click **Folder**. Name the folder **A Test**.

3. Leave Windows Explorer open.

4. Click **Start**, point to **All Programs**, point to **Accessories**, and then click **Paint**.

5. Create a cheerful drawing of any type. Click **File**, and then click **Save As**. Name your file **My Test Paint File 1**, select **24–bit Bitmap** as the Save as type, select **A Test** in the Save in list box, and then click **Save**.

6. Repeat Step 5 three times, changing the "1" in the file name to "**2**," "**3**," and "**4**," respectively.

7. Exit Paint.

8. Return to Windows Explorer and open the **A Test** folder. If necessary, click **View**, **Details**. Note the timestamps in the Date Modified column of the files in that folder.

9. Click **Start**, point to **All Programs**, point to **Microsoft Office**, point to **Microsoft Office Tools**, and then click **Microsoft Office Picture Manager**. If necessary, click **OK** in the File Types dialog box. Your screen should resemble Figure 8-10.

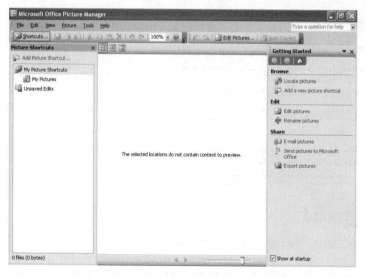

**Figure 8-10**    Microsoft Office Picture Manager

10. The Picture Shortcuts on the left side of your screen are the default shortcut locations. Click the **Locate pictures** link in the Getting Started pane on the right side of your screen. If prompted with a Look in text box, accept the default and click **OK**. Wait while Microsoft Office Picture Manager locates new pictures.

11. Note that the Picture Shortcuts on the left side of your screen have changed to include the **A Test** folder. If your screen does not show the A Test folder, click the **Add Picture Shortcut** link, navigate to and select **A Test** in the Look in list box, and then click **Add**. Your screen should resemble Figure 8-11. It's in Thumbnail view by default.

12. At the bottom of the screen, note the arrows to the right of the "My Test Paint File 1" file name. Click the **right arrow** three times while watching the focus of the software move from file to file in the pane above. Move the slider to the right of the arrows, to the left, and to the right again to see the changes in the Thumbnail View display.

13. Click **View**, **Show File Names** from the menu to remove the check mark. Note that the file names disappear from the middle pane of your screen. Click **View**, **Show File Names** again to restore the names.

14. Click the first thumbnail. In the Picture Shortcuts pane on the left, note that there are no entries under the Unsaved Edits category. Click **Picture**, **Brightness and Contrast** from the menu. In the Brightness and Contrast pane on the right, experiment with the effects of the different sliders. As soon as you begin to play with these sliders, "Unsaved Edits" in the left pane becomes "Unsaved Edits (1)."

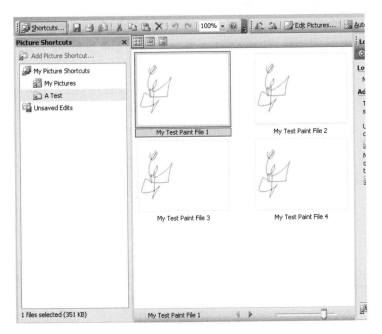

**Figure 8-11**  A shortcut has been added

15. Click **Unsaved Edits (1)** in the left pane. The middle pane now shows only the current unsaved file on which you're working. Press **Ctrl+S**. The file is saved back to its original location and the "Unsaved Edits (1)" text goes back to "Unsaved Edits."

16. Click the **A Test** shortcut, and notice that My Test Paint File 1 has changed. Click the Single Picture View icon at the top of the pane to show only this one changed file in the middle pane.

17. Return to Windows Explorer, and open the **A Test** folder. Note that My Test Paint File 1 has a new timestamp. This new timestamp is proof that you have changed your file.

18. Return to Microsoft Office Picture Manager, and explore other pictures and images on your computer.

19. Exit Microsoft Office Picture Manager, close Windows Explorer, and log off.

## Certification Objectives

Objectives for Microsoft Exam #70-272: Supporting Users and Troubleshooting Desktop Applications on a Microsoft Windows XP Operating System:

Although this lab provides knowledge and skills desktop support technicians should have to fulfill their job responsibilities, it doesn't map directly to any MCDST certification objectives.

## Review Questions

1. In Microsoft Office Picture Manager, you can manipulate both drawings and photographs. True or False?

2. By default, the Add Picture Shortcut dialog box contains the _____ folder in its Look in list box.

3. Describe the common shortcuts in the Picture Shortcuts pane in Microsoft Office Picture Manager.

4. The Unsaved Edits shortcut houses files you have saved while Microsoft Office Picture Manager is open. True or False?

5. In Microsoft Office Picture Manager, you can compress pictures for use in Web pages and _____ .

# 9

# CONFIGURE, CUSTOMIZE, AND MIGRATE TO OUTLOOK

## Labs included in this chapter:

➤ Lab 9.1 Sending and Receiving E-mails

➤ Lab 9.2 Working with the Outlook Calendar

➤ Lab 9.3 Working with the Contacts Feature in Outlook

➤ Lab 9.4 Exploring the Options Dialog Box in Outlook

| Microsoft MCDST Exam #70-272 Objectives | |
|---|---|
| Objective | Lab |
| Manage Outlook data, including configuring, importing, and exporting data, and repairing corrupted data. | 9.1, 9.2, 9.3, 9.4 |

## Lab 9.1 Sending and Receiving E-mails

### Objectives

The goal of this lab is to learn how to quickly sort and organize incoming messages in Outlook so that you can have information displayed in a manner that works for you. Although these tasks might seem simple, they are common skills that most end users want to master, and they will be the basis of many questions you're asked.

### Materials Required

This lab requires the following:

➤ A computer running Microsoft Windows XP

➤ Administrative rights on the computer

➤ An e-mail account on your computer that has been set up to work with Outlook

➤ Internet or intranet access (depending on how your e-mail account accesses e-mail messages)

➤ A partner with the same Outlook rights and permissions that you have

Estimated completion time: 15 minutes

### Activity Background

In this lab, you discover that Outlook has basic presentation options that end users consider necessities in their work environment. When they inadvertently cause these options to disappear or not function as before, they will call you for help and most likely be feeling frantic.

### Activity

1. Log on to the computer. You need to log on with administrative rights.

2. Start Outlook by clicking the **Outlook** icon on the Quick Launch toolbar, as shown in Figure 9-1.

If you don't see the Quick Launch toolbar, right-click the taskbar, point to Toolbars, and then click Quick Launch.

**Figure 9-1** The Quick Launch toolbar

3. Outlook appears on your screen and might look similar to Figure 9-2. (The screen display can vary, depending on how you set up Outlook and options you might have used since then.) Press **Alt+F1** several times to watch the navigation pane disappear and reappear.

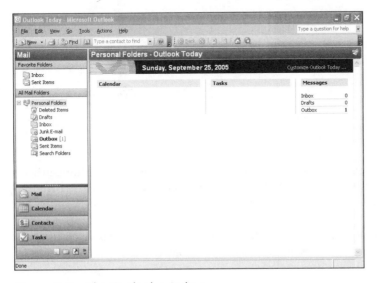

**Figure 9-2** The Outlook window

4. Press **Ctrl+N**, and set the toolbars on the screen to your preference. Your screen should resemble Figure 9-3. In the To field, enter your own e-mail address. (If you click the To label instead of its text box, you open the Select Names dialog box. In this dialog box, you can select individual recipients or distribution lists for the To field.) In the Subject field, type **First Lab 9.1 e-mail**. In the body, type **First Lab 9.1 e-maiil** (including the typo in the last word). Press the **spacebar**, and notice that Outlook highlights the misspelling of the word with a red wavy line. Right-click the line, and then click **mail**.

5. On the menu bar, click **Insert**, point to **Picture**, and then click **From File**. (*Note*: If the Picture suboptions are dimmed, Outlook is building the e-mail in plain text, which does not support inserting figures. To fix this problem, click the **Message Format** list arrow, and then click **HTML**.) Navigate to **My Pictures**, if necessary. Double-click **Sample Pictures**, select a picture in the folder, and then click **Insert**. The image is inserted in—rather than attached to—the e-mail.

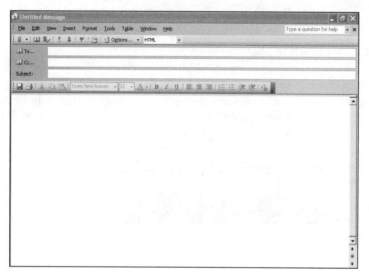

**Figure 9-3** Starting an e-mail

6. Click **Send**. The window closes. In the navigation pane, notice that your e-mail is now in the Outbox. The existence of an e-mail—or multiple e-mails—is indicated by a number in brackets next to the word "Outbox."

For users with always-on connections, clicking Send, as in Step 6, automatically sends the e-mail, unless the end user has set options otherwise.

**NOTE**

7. Repeat Steps 4 through 6 three times, changing each instance of "First" to **Second**, **Third**, and **Fourth**. For the fourth e-mail, attach a file in addition to inserting a picture. To do so, click **Insert**, **File** from the menu, select a small text or Word file from the My Documents folder, and then click **Insert**.

8. Connect to the Internet or intranet. For help in connecting to your ISP or the server handling your e-mail, contact your instructor.

9. In Outlook, click the **Send/Receive** button on the Standard toolbar. (You can also press **F9** to send your e-mails.) Wait for the e-mails to be sent and then received by your computer.

10. In the navigation pane in Outlook, click **Inbox**, if necessary. In the Inbox in the middle of your screen, note that the e-mails are sorted by a variety of headers. Right-click the **From** header and read the content of the shortcut menu, shown in Figure 9-4.

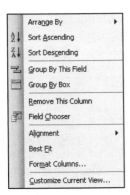

**Figure 9-4** Choices for organizing your e-mail

11. Right-click the **From** header again, point to **Arrange By**, and then click **Subject**. Notice how the ordering of your e-mails changes. Right-click the **From** header again, point to **Arrange By**, and then click **Attachments**. The ordering of your e-mails changes again.

12. Explore the other options available via this shortcut menu.

13. Time permitting, have your partner send you some e-mails with a variety of attachments so that you can have practice working with e-mails.

14. Close Outlook, and log off.

## Certification Objectives

Objectives for Microsoft Exam #70-272: Supporting Users and Troubleshooting Desktop Applications on a Microsoft Windows XP Operating System:

➤ Manage Outlook data, including configuring, importing, and exporting data, and repairing corrupted data.

## Review Questions

1. The _____ toolbar contains, by default, an icon you can use to open Outlook.
   a. Quick Launch
   b. Outlook
   c. navigation
   d. reading pane

2. What are the characteristics of a plain text e-mail?

3. In Outlook, the reading pane can be docked on the left side of your screen. True or False?

4. List three ways in which you can sort messages in Outlook.

5. Briefly describe the content of the navigation pane.

---

# LAB 9.2 WORKING WITH THE OUTLOOK CALENDAR

## Objectives

The goal of this lab is to become familiar with Outlook's Calendar feature. Although some users in your organization might prefer to use day planners and perhaps personal data assistants (PDAs) to organize their workdays, their numbers are thinning rapidly. Whether your end users are organizing their own workdays or a work schedule for the entire team, they'll find the Calendar feature useful.

## Materials Required

This lab requires the following:

➤ A computer running Microsoft Windows XP

➤ Administrative rights on the computer

➤ An e-mail account on your computer that has been set up to work with Outlook

➤ Computer speakers with the volume turned on

Estimated completion time: **15 minutes**

## Activity Background

In this lab, you discover what many power users already know—the Calendar feature of Outlook lets you concentrate on your job, not on manually tracking the minute-to-minute details of your workday.

**LAB ACTIVITY**

## Activity

1. Log on to the computer. You need to log on with administrative rights.

2. Start Outlook by clicking the **Outlook** icon on the Quick Launch toolbar. Click **Calendar** in the navigation pane. Your screen should look similar to Figure 9-5.

3. In the Calendar pane, find the first time slot after the current time on your computer. For example, if the current time on your computer is 9:45 a.m., find the 10:00 a.m. slot on the Calendar. Note that each hour slot is divided into two rows. Each row corresponds with one half-hour of the listed time.

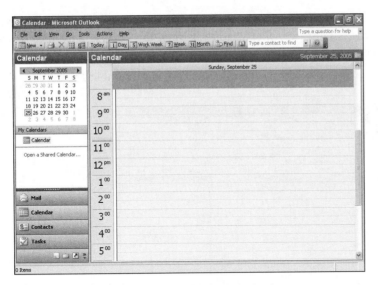

**Figure 9-5**    The Calendar interface in Outlook

> Double-click the first half-hour row to open the Appointment dialog box, shown in Figure 9-6.

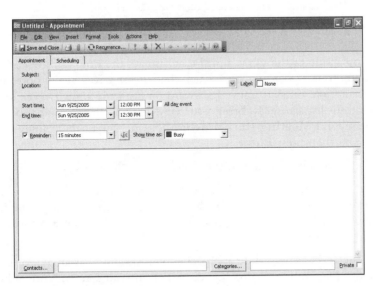

**Figure 9-6**    The Appointment dialog box

> 4. On the Appointment tab, notice that your appointment is, by default, one-half hour long. Click the second **End time** list arrow, and then click *time* **(1 hour)**. The *time* depends on your computer's clock time.

5. Click the sound icon, which opens the Reminder Sound dialog box. You can accept the default .wav file, or you can click the Browse button to select another .wav file, if you have one on your computer. Click **OK**.

6. Click the **Scheduling** tab. Your screen should resemble Figure 9-7.

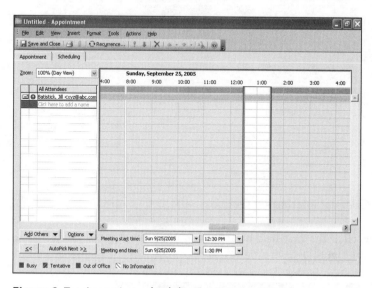

**Figure 9-7**   Accessing scheduling options

7. On the right side of the tab is a grid that displays the hours of the current day. Your appointment is on this grid. Click the left list arrow at the bottom of this grid multiple times to move backward on the time scale. Do the same with the right list arrow. To bring your view back to the current appointment, click the second **Meeting start time** list box, increment the minute by one number, and then press **Enter**.

8. Click the **Zoom** list arrow, and then click **50% (Week View)**.

9. Leave the dialog box open until the meeting time has passed. Notice that you didn't hear the reminder sound for this meeting. Set the meeting time for a few minutes past your current clock time, and then click the **Save and Close** button to return to Outlook.

10. When your appointment time approaches, you should hear an audio reminder and see the 1 Reminder dialog box displayed on your screen. Notice the Due in time setting in this dialog box. Ignore the reminder and wait one more minute. You hear another audio warning. Notice that the Due in time value in this dialog box has changed again; it continues doing so as your attendance to this task goes overdue.

11. Click the **Dismiss** button.

12. Close Outlook, and log off.

## Certification Objectives

Objectives for Microsoft Exam #70-272: Supporting Users and Troubleshooting Desktop Applications on a Microsoft Windows XP Operating System:

➤ Manage Outlook data, including configuring, importing, and exporting data, and repairing corrupted data.

## Review Questions

1. You must be connected to the Internet or intranet for Outlook's Calendar feature to work. True or False?

2. In the Appointment dialog box, you can access more than one week of schedules in the time grid. True or False?

3. In Outlook, what is the name of the audio file that plays by default to remind you of an appointment?

4. What are the buttons in the 1 Reminder dialog box?

5. In the 1 Reminder dialog box, you can click the Snooze button to select a time frame after which you want to be reminded of an appointment. True or False?

# LAB 9.3 WORKING WITH THE CONTACTS FEATURE IN OUTLOOK

## Objectives

The goal of this lab is to explore the basic elements of Outlook's Contacts feature. In the past, a Rolodex card organizer was all you needed to keep details—such as names and phone numbers—of your business contacts in order. Now, however, with the addition of e-mail addresses, remote address locations, and multiple phone numbers, a card organizer isn't as useful as it once was. This explosion of information for individual contacts makes Outlook's Contacts feature indispensable.

## Materials Required

This lab requires the following:

➤ A computer running Microsoft Windows XP

➤ Administrative rights on the computer

➤ An e-mail account on your computer that has been set up to work with Outlook

Estimated completion time: 15 minutes

## Activity Background

In this lab, you discover the wide variety of information that can be stored about your end users' contacts. The more you can nudge your end users into using this option to organize information, the more productive they can be.

**ACTIVITY**

1. Log on to the computer. You need to log on with administrative rights.

2. Start Outlook by clicking the **Outlook** icon on the Quick Launch toolbar.

3. Click the **Contacts** option in the navigation pane.

4. Click the **New** button on the Standard toolbar to open the Contact dialog box, shown in Figure 9-8.

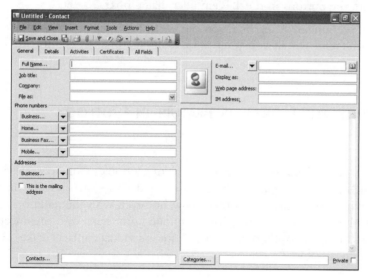

**Figure 9-8**   Creating a new contact

5. Type a name into the Full Name text box. Click the **Full Name** button to open the Check Full Name dialog box. Notice that some text boxes are already filled in. Fill in the remaining text boxes, and then click **OK**.

6. In the Phone numbers section, click the **Business** button to open the Check Phone Number dialog box. Fill in the options, and then click **OK**. Click the **Business** list arrow, make a selection, and then type a number in the respective text box.

7. Click the **Add Contact Picture** button, which is in the top middle of the General tab. Double-click **Sample Pictures**, and then double-click **Blue hills.jpg** (or another file of your choice). The image is then displayed in the General tab.

If your company gives access to employee ID pictures, using these pictures in this feature can prove useful for your end users.

8. Click the **E-mail** list arrow, make a selection, and then type an e-mail address. Click the **Details** tab and fill in at least three fields. Click the **Save and Close** button. Explore the options on the other tabs, as time permits.

9. Repeat Steps 4 through 8 for at least three more contacts, making sure each contact has a last name that begins with a different letter than the others.

10. On the far right side of the Contact pane title bar, Outlook shows the alphabetical span of contacts in your Contact list, as shown in Figure 9-9. Notice the list of letters down the right side of your screen. Click the letters corresponding to the last names of your contacts. The focus in the Contact list changes as you click each letter. If your Contact list were made up of many hundreds of names, this sorting feature would help you move through those names easily.

11. In the Contact list, right-click one of the names, and then click **New Appointment with Contact**. This opens the Appointment dialog box, which you already explored in Lab 9.2. Close the dialog box, and then click **No** to the resulting prompt.

As your end users become more familiar with Outlook, they'll find more interrelated elements between items in the navigation pane.

12. Right-click another name in the list, point to **Link**, and then click **Items**. The Link Items to Contact dialog box opens. As you send e-mails to and receive e-mails from the current contact, those e-mails would be listed in this dialog box. Click **Cancel**.

13. Right-click another name in the list, point to **Link**, and then click **File** to open the Choose a File dialog box. Double-click a picture file in this dialog box to open the Journal Entry dialog box. In this dialog box, you can build a journal entry for later use. Close the dialog box, and click **No** to the resulting prompt.

14. Explore the other options in this view, as time permits.

15. Close Outlook, and log off.

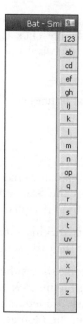

**Figure 9-9**   Alphabetical range of contacts' last names

## Certification Objectives

Objectives for Microsoft Exam #70-272: Supporting Users and Troubleshooting Desktop Applications on a Microsoft Windows XP Operating System:

➤ Manage Outlook data, including configuring, importing, and exporting data, and repairing corrupted data.

## Review Questions

1. List and briefly describe two tabs in the Contact dialog box.

2. The Add Contact Picture options in the Contact dialog box can be used to display a .jpg or .wav file. True or False?

3. The Detailed Address Cards view displays all the respective fields for a contact, even if those fields contain no information. True or False?

4. Right-clicking a name in the Contacts list in Outlook and then clicking _____ starts a new e-mail to that person.

5. List three of the options available under Current View in Outlook's Contacts feature.

## LAB 9.4 EXPLORING THE OPTIONS DIALOG BOX IN OUTLOOK

### Objectives

The goal of this lab is to become familiar with the choices available in the Options dialog box in Outlook. When your end users become familiar with the basic uses of Outlook—receiving and sending e-mail, using the calendar, and organizing contacts—they'll become more sophisticated at making selections in this dialog box.

### Materials Required

This lab requires the following:

➤ A computer running Microsoft Windows XP

➤ Administrative rights on the computer

➤ An e-mail account on your computer that has been set up to work with Outlook

➤ Completion of Labs 9.1 through 9.3

Estimated completion time: 15 minutes

### Activity Background

In this lab, you discover that the appearance and formatting of information in Outlook can be customized to the end user's preference. Knowing these options inside and out can save you time in your workday—your users will generate plenty of questions based on them.

**LAB ACTIVITY**

### ACTIVITY

1. Log on to the computer. You need to log on with administrative rights.

2. Start Outlook by clicking the **Outlook** icon on the Quick Launch toolbar.

3. Click **Tools**, **Options** from the menu. In the Options dialog box, click the **Preferences** tab, if necessary. Your screen should resemble Figure 9-10.

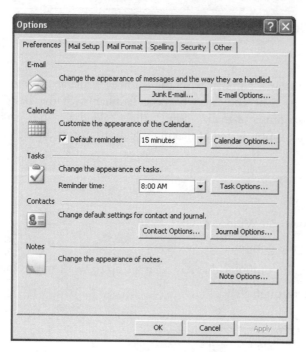

**Figure 9-10** The Options dialog box

4. Click each button in the E-mail section in turn, noting the options you can set. If you click the Junk E-mail button, your screen resembles Figure 9-11. If you click the E-mail Options button, your screen resembles Figure 9-12. Close the resulting dialog box after exploring each set of options.

5. Click the **Calendar Options** button, and click to clear all the Calendar work week check boxes, except Thursday's. Click **OK**, and then click **OK**.

6. Click the **Calendar** option in the navigation pane. Click **View**, **Work Week** from the menu. Notice that the main pane in the window still displays only one day—the day you specified as the "entire work week" in the Options dialog box.

7. Click **Tools**, **Options** from the menu. Click the **Mail Format** tab. Click **HTML** in the Compose in this message format list box, if necessary, and then click the **Fonts** button. Click the first **Choose Font** button, change the font to one you prefer, and then click **20** in the Size list box. Click **OK** three times.

8. Click the **Mail** option in the navigation pane. Open one of the e-mails that you wrote and sent in Lab 9.1. Observe the default font that was used, and close the e-mail. Press **Ctrl+N**, and then click in the e-mail's body text box. Type a line of text, noticing the style and size of the new font selection.

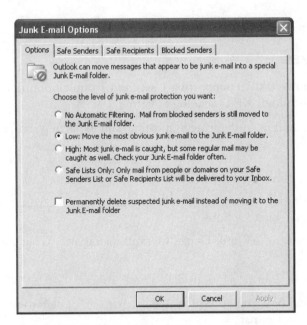

**Figure 9-11**   The Junk E-mail Options dialog box

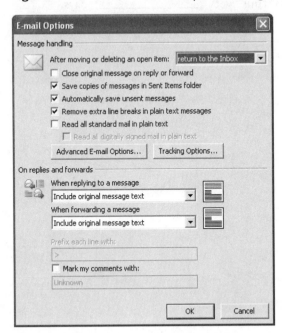

**Figure 9-12** The E-mail Options dialog box

9.  Close the e-mail without saving the changes.

10.  Explore other options in the Options dialog box as time permits.

11. Close Outlook, and log off.

## Certification Objectives

Objectives for Microsoft Exam #70-272: Supporting Users and Troubleshooting Desktop Applications on a Microsoft Windows XP Operating System:

➤ Manage Outlook data, including configuring, importing, and exporting data, and repairing corrupted data.

## Review Questions

1. You can open the Options dialog box by clicking _____ on the menu bar and then clicking Options.

2. What are the four tabs in the Junk E-mail Options dialog box? What are their options?

3. How do you open the Journal Options dialog box?

4. In the Options dialog box, you access the _____ tab to make selections for encrypted e-mail.

5. By default, AutoArchive runs every _____ days.

# CONFIGURE AND TROUBLESHOOT DEVICES AND CONNECTIVITY FOR APPLICATIONS

---

## Labs included in this chapter:

➤ Lab 10.1 Working with Device Manager

➤ Lab 10.2 Understanding Driver Signing

➤ Lab 10.3 Cleaning up a Hard Drive

➤ Lab 10.4 Working with a Printer

---

| Microsoft MCDST Exam #70-272 Objectives | |
|---|---|
| Objective | Lab |
| Identify and troubleshoot problems with locally attached devices. Indications of such problems include application errors. | 10.1, 10.2, 10.3, 10.4 |

## LAB 10.1 WORKING WITH DEVICE MANAGER

### Objectives

The goal of this lab is to become familiar with Device Manager. Device Manager is a tool you can use to interact—at the driver level—with the hardware attached to your computer. Whether you are troubleshooting over the network or at an end user's computer, checking Device Manager is your first stop when pieces of hardware stop working.

### Materials Required

This lab requires the following:

➤ A computer running Microsoft Windows XP

➤ Administrative rights on the computer on an account that does not have a password

➤ A working keyboard on your system

Estimated completion time: 15 minutes

### Activity Background

In this lab, you find that Device Manager is an indispensable tool. From batteries to monitors, it's the place to go when end users' work environments stop working.

LAB ACTIVITY

### ACTIVITY

1. Log on to the computer. You need to log on with administrative rights.

2. Click **Start, Control Panel**. If necessary, click **Switch to Classic View**, and then double-click **System**.

3. Click the **Hardware** tab, and then click the **Device Manager** button.

4. Double-click **Keyboards**, and then double-click your keyboard in the expanded list. The Properties dialog box for this device opens, as shown in Figure 10-1. Notice that Device Manager has determined that the keyboard is working correctly.

5. Close the Properties dialog box and then close Device Manager.

6. Unplug the keyboard from the back of your computer. Click **Start**, point to **All Programs**, point to **Accessories**, and then click **Notepad**. Try to type in the window. Notice that no text appears. Close the Notepad window.

7. In the System Properties dialog box, click **Device Manager**. Click the **Hardware** tab, and then click the **Device Manager** button. Double-click **Keyboards**, and then double-click your keyboard in the expanded list. Note

**Figure 10-1** Checking the status of a device

that Device Manager has not recognized that the keyboard is missing. The reason is that on startup, Device Manager recognized the keyboard. It doesn't "unrecognize" the keyboard until you restart your computer.

8. Close all the open windows and then restart your computer. Watch the screen as the computer restarts. While the screen is still displaying white text and a black background, you can see "Keyboard failure" and other information. Wait while Windows XP continues to load.

The startup information that's displayed on your screen before the GUI can be a valuable troubleshooting tip. Make use of it whenever possible.

**NOTE**

9. Log on to the computer. You need to log on with administrative rights.

10. Open Device Manager. Your screen should resemble Figure 10-2. Notice that Device Manager doesn't even list the keyboard—failure or not—because it didn't detect it on startup. This oversight is a limitation of Device Manager.

11. Close Device Manager and any other open windows.

12. Shut down your computer, reconnect the keyboard, and then restart the computer.

13. Log on to the computer. You need to log on with administrative rights.

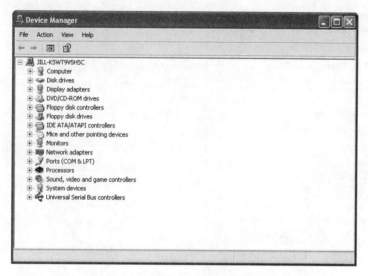

**Figure 10-2**   Device Manager doesn't list the keyboard

14. Open Notepad and confirm that your keyboard works. Disconnect the keyboard. Confirm that your keyboard does not work. Reconnect the keyboard and confirm that your keyboard again works.

15. Experiment with other hardware devices, as time permits.

16. Close all open windows, and log off.

## Certification Objectives

Objectives for Microsoft Exam #70-272: Supporting Users and Troubleshooting Desktop Applications on a Microsoft Windows XP Operating System:

➤ Identify and troubleshoot problems with locally attached devices. Indications of such problems include application errors.

## Review Questions

1. A device connected to your computer always shows up in Device Manager. True or False?

2. What is the click sequence for opening Device Manager from the Start menu?

3. If your mouse is disconnected, your keyboard can still work. True or False?

4. You can access Device Manager through the _____ tab of the System Properties dialog box.

5. Where in your system are driver files stored?

# LAB 10.2 UNDERSTANDING DRIVER SIGNING

## Objectives

The goal of this lab is to become familiar with driver signing in Windows. When a driver on your computer has been signed by Microsoft, you know it was tested to meet certain Microsoft requirements. If you're working on a computer with a fresh installation of Windows XP, you probably have only Microsoft-approved drivers on your system. However, when you use your system and download files from the Internet, you can no longer be positive that all drivers on your system are signed. Fortunately, to double-check the signature integrity of existing drivers on your system, you can use the Sigverif command.

## Materials Required

This lab requires the following:

➤ A computer running Microsoft Windows XP

➤ Administrative rights on the computer

➤ At least one non-signed driver installed on the system

➤ Internet access

**10**

Estimated completion time: 15 minutes

## Activity Background

In this lab, you get to use the Sigverif command. Using the command prompt window might seem intimidating at first, but after you get used to it, you'll wonder how you ever lived without it. In addition, you have the opportunity to save the results of this command's search to a text file, which should prove useful later if you need to e-mail the content to another DST on your team.

LAB ACTIVITY

## ACTIVITY

1. Log on to the computer. You need to log on with administrative rights.

2. Click **Start**, **Run**, type **sigverif**, and then press **Enter**. Your screen should resemble Figure 10-3.

3. Click **Start**. Wait while Windows XP scans the files. Depending on the software and files installed on your computer, you might see results similar to Figure 10-4.

**Figure 10-3** Using Sigverif

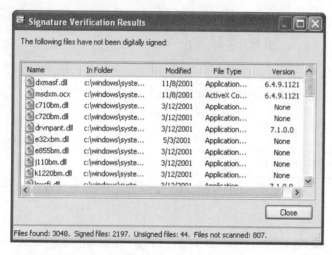

**Figure 10-4** Scan results

4. To view the entire text file this command generates (which includes both signed and unsigned drivers), open Windows Explorer and navigate to this path: **C:\WINDOWS\SIGVERIF**.

5. Right-click the file, point to **Open With**, and then click **WordPad**. The results on your computer will likely differ, but your screen should look similar to Figure 10-5. Scroll through and skim the document's contents. The file is usually quite large.

6. On the author's computer, one of the unsigned drivers was mdigraph.dll. If you have an unsigned driver in your version of Sigverif, use it in place of "mdigraph.dll" in this step. Connect to the Internet and point your browser to **www.google.com**, type **mdigraph.dll** in the Search box, and then press **Enter**.

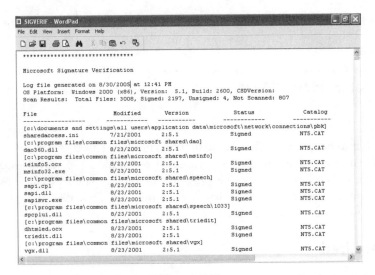

**Figure 10-5**  Reading the Sigverif file

7. Click a few of the returned links. From your readings, you'll learn that the file is a Microsoft Office driver. This information is helpful when you and your teammates are deciding what to do—if anything—with this particular driver.

8. Connect to **www.microsoft.com** and perform the same search. Read the results of your search.

9. Disconnect from the Internet. Close the WordPad window, and log off.

## Certification Objectives

Objectives for Microsoft Exam #70-272: Supporting Users and Troubleshooting Desktop Applications on a Microsoft Windows XP Operating System:

➤ Identify and troubleshoot problems with locally attached devices. Indications of such problems include application errors.

## Review Questions

1. To check for driver integrity on your system, you can type _____ in the Run dialog box.

2. Drivers that Windows XP installs cannot be scanned for digital signatures. True or False?

3. The Sigverif file can show both signed and unsigned drivers. True or False?

4. The file extension _____ is a common file extension for drivers produced by a Sigverif scan.

5. The Sigverif file can list files that aren't currently installed on your computer. True or False?

---

## LAB 10.3 CLEANING UP A HARD DRIVE

### Objectives

The goal of this lab is to become comfortable with removing elements that take up space on your hard drive. Even though hard drives are getting larger—and less expensive—operating systems, applications, and end users' files are keeping up with their capability to fill those hard drives. Knowing how to pare back a hard drive's contents with Disk Cleanup and other techniques can be useful in your career as a DST.

### Materials Required

This lab requires the following:

➤ A computer running Microsoft Windows XP

➤ Administrative rights on the computer

➤ An installed program, such as a game, that can be uninstalled from your computer

➤ Enough use of the computer on the Internet to create files in the folders listed in Step 5

Estimated completion time: **15 minutes**

### Activity Background

Workstation hard drives—whether 40, 80, or more GB—can fill up fast, even when your company uses thinner clients. Knowing how to get in and fix the problem of a hard drive running out of space makes you an instant hero (and gives you the opportunity to ask your co-worker why he or she has so many vacation photos on the company's workstation or is playing unauthorized games on company time).

**LAB ACTIVITY**

### ACTIVITY

1. Log on to the computer. You need to log on with administrative rights.

2. Open Notepad. Create a file and save it under My Documents with a name of your choosing. Close Notepad.

3. Right-click **Start**, click **Explore**, navigate to **C:\Documents and Settings\\***Your User Name***\My Documents**, and delete the file. This step ensures that you have something in the Recycle Bin on your computer.

4. In Windows Explorer, right-click **Local Disk (C:)**, and then click **Properties**. Your screen should resemble Figure 10-6. Note the amount of free space you have on your computer. Click **OK**.

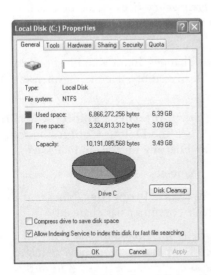

**Figure 10-6**   Disk information

5. Navigate in Windows Explorer to the following locations and note the content and size of the files in each folder:

   a. C:\Documents and Settings\*Your User Name*\Cookies

   b. C:\Documents and Settings\*Your User Name*\Local Settings\History

   c. C:\Documents and Settings\*Your User Name*\Local Settings\Temp

   d. C:\Documents and Settings\*Your User Name*\Local Settings\Temporary Internet Files

   e. Recycle Bin

6. To run Disk Cleanup, click **Start**, **Run**, type **cleanmgr**, and press **Enter**. Your screen should resemble Figure 10-7.

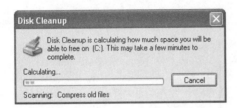

**Figure 10-7**   Using Disk Cleanup

7. When the Disk Cleanup for (C:) dialog box opens, click the **Disk Cleanup** tab, if necessary, and then click to clear the **Downloaded Program Files** check box. Leave the Temporary Internet Files check box selected. Click the **Recycle Bin** check box and the **Temporary files** check box. Click **OK**, and then click **Yes**. Wait while Disk Cleanup runs through your files, making deletions.

8. Check the folders listed in Step 5 for changes. Items a and b show no changes, but items c through e are empty or nearly empty, depending on your computer's settings.

9. Open Internet Explorer by clicking **Start**, **Internet Explorer**. Click **Tools**, **Internet Options** from the menu. Click the **Delete Cookies** button, and then click **OK**. Then click the **Clear History** button, and click **Yes**.

10. Check folders a and b in Step 5 for changes.

11. Right-click **Local Disk (C:)**, and then click **Properties**. Note that the amount of free space you have on your computer has changed.

12. Navigate to **C:\Program Files\***Title of the Program That You Can Delete*. Right-click the folder, and then click **Properties**. Note how much space the files are taking on your computer. You could delete the files from this folder, but you should not do so in this manner. The removal might be incomplete, and it might also delete files needed by other programs.

13. Click **Start**, **Control Panel**, and double-click **Add or Remove Program**. Click the program in question, and then click the **Change/Remove** button. Click the **Uninstall** button, as shown in Figure 10-8, and follow the prompts to the end of the process.

**NOTE**     Depending on how you installed Windows XP and/or the program you are deleting, the process in Step 13 might differ slightly.

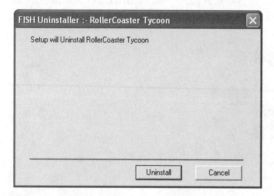

**Figure 10-8**     Removing a program

14. In Explorer, right-click **Local Disk (C:)**, and then click **Properties**. Note that the amount of free space on your computer has changed.

15. Close all open windows, and log off.

## Certification Objectives

Objectives for Microsoft Exam #70-272: Supporting Users and Troubleshooting Desktop Applications on a Microsoft Windows XP Operating System:

➤ Identify and troubleshoot problems with locally attached devices. Indications of such problems include application errors.

## Review Questions

1. Where does Windows XP save application files by default?

2. What are the tabs of the Local Disk (C:) Properties dialog box?

3. Disk Cleanup can be run from both the GUI and the command line. True or False?

4. In the Internet Options dialog box, the Delete Cookies button is found in the _____ tab.

5. Via the Internet Options dialog box, what is the maximum number of days you can select to keep pages in history?

   a. 10

   b. 99

   c. 100

   d. 999

**10**

# LAB 10.4 WORKING WITH A PRINTER

## Objectives

The goal of this lab is to become proficient at recognizing problems that end users often have with printers. Although printers might seem a bit unglamorous to master, don't count on an end user with a deadline to share your disinterest. Printing is the final step in many important business tasks.

## Materials Required

This lab requires the following:

➤ A computer running Microsoft Windows XP

➤ Administrative rights on the computer

➤ No installed printers on the computer

➤ A printer with the correct printer cartridge, paper in the printer, a printer cable, and the installation CD that comes with the printer

Estimated completion time: 15 minutes

## Activity Background

In this lab, you find out what busy corporate workers already know—printing is important. When the person trying to print is a vice president on the way to a meeting, printing is *really* important. Don't flub your chance to be the hero. Learn the basics of printing from a workstation to an attached printer, and you can quickly master the intricacies of doing so across the network.

### ACTIVITY

1. Log on to the computer. You need to log on with administrative rights. Click **Start**, **Control Panel**, and then double-click **Printers and Faxes**. If any printers are installed, right-click the appropriate icon, and then click **Delete**.

2. Open Word by clicking **Start**, pointing to **All Programs**, pointing to **Microsoft Office**, and then clicking **Microsoft Office Word 2003**. Close the Task Pane, if necessary.

3. Type your name and then click the **Print** button. The Save As dialog box opens. Notice the Save as type list box, shown in Figure 10-9. Because no printer is installed, Word is trying to "print" the document to a file in lieu of performing a physical print. Click **Cancel**. Close Word.

**Figure 10-9**   Notice the file type

4. Attach your uninstalled printer to the computer and turn on the power to the printer. Your computer does not recognize the printer. Turn the power back off and back on. Still nothing happens. Leave the printer turned on.

5. Click **Start**, **Turn Off Computer**, **Restart**. Log in. You should see a screen similar to Figure 10-10. Click **Cancel**. (You didn't think you'd install the easy way, did you?)

6. Insert your installation CD into its drive. Your computer automatically recognizes the CD and displays a window similar to Figure 10-11. Close the window.

**Figure 10-10**   New hardware was detected

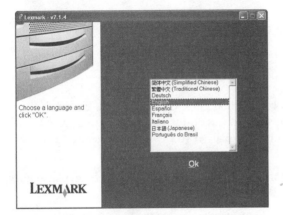

**Figure 10-11**   Installation screen

7. Right-click **Start**, click **Explore**, and find your CD drive letter, usually preceded by the printer manufacturer's name, as shown in Figure 10-12.

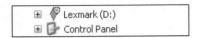

**Figure 10-12**   Printer name with the drive letter

8. Double-click the folder. In the right pane, look for the SETUP file (of type "Application"), and then double-click it. You return to the same wizard you saw in Figure 10-11. Follow the prompts until the printer is installed.

9. Open Word, close the Task Pane, type your name, and then click the **Print** button. The page should print on your newly installed printer.

10. Without turning off the printer, disconnect its cable from the back of your computer. Press **Ctrl+P**, and then click **OK**. After a few moments, you see a message stating that the document failed to print.

11. On your status bar, double-click the printer icon to see the status of the print job, similar to Figure 10-13.

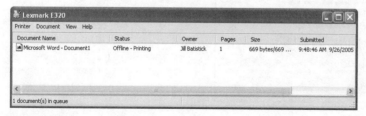

**Figure 10-13**     Status of the print job

 From the Printer menu in this dialog box, you can also pause and resume print jobs.

**NOTE**

12. Right-click the print job, and then click **Cancel**. Click **Yes** to the resulting prompt. Notice that the status changes during the deletion process. Close the printer window. Reattach your printer to the computer, and press **Ctrl+P** again. The page prints.

13. Click **Start**, **Control Panel**, and then double-click **Printers and Faxes**. Your printer is displayed in this window.

14. Right-click your printer's icon, and note the many options that you have through the pop-up menu. Click **Printing Preferences**. Explore the tabs in the Printing Preferences dialog box. Click **OK**.

15. Close all open windows.

16. Remove your installation CD, and log off.

## Certification Objectives

Objectives for Microsoft Exam #70-272: Supporting Users and Troubleshooting Desktop Applications on a Microsoft Windows XP Operating System:

➤ Identify and troubleshoot problems with locally attached devices. Indications of such problems include application errors.

## Review Questions

1. If you try to print on a computer that has no printer installed or accessible—either directly connected to the machine or over the network—your computer might attempt to save the file with a(n)_____ extension.

2. When you right-click a print job in a printer window, what are your choices on the pop-up menu?

3. You can open the Printers and Faxes window via Control Panel. True or False?

4. More than one printer can be listed in the Printers and Faxes window. True or False?

5. You can set the dithering option for a laser printer in the _____ tab of the Printing Preferences dialog box.

**10**

# RESOLVE FOLDER AND FILE ISSUES

## Labs included in this chapter:

➤ Lab 11.1 Exploring File Access on a Workstation

➤ Lab 11.2 Working with Lost Information or Files

➤ Lab 11.3 Working with Quotas

➤ Lab 11.4 Working with Permissions

| Microsoft MCDST Exam #70-272 Objectives | |
|---|---|
| Objective | Lab |
| Configure and troubleshoot file system access and file permission problems on multiboot computers. | 11.4 |
| Configure and troubleshoot application access on a multiple user client computer. | 11.2 |
| Troubleshoot insufficient user permissions and rights. | 11.1, 11.2, 11.3 |

## Lab 11.1 Exploring File Access on a Workstation

### Objectives

The goal of this lab is to become familiar with file access on your workstation via sharing. You might have multiple users on your workstation, but you might not want all of them to have the same access. As companies downsize and resources such as workstations are used by multiple end users—even within the same work shift—knowing the basics of sharing and related options can help you manage their workdays.

### Materials Required

This lab requires the following:

➤ A computer that runs Microsoft Windows XP and is capable of booting to another operating system

➤ An account with administrative rights on the computer

Estimated completion time: 15 minutes

### Activity Background

In this lab, you discover that sharing can be enforced in different ways. Knowing the ins and outs of sharing is helpful when an end user needs to open a file, but can't.

LAB ACTIVITY

### Activity

1. Log on to the computer. You need to log on with administrative rights.

2. Confirm your file system by doing the following: Right-click **Start**, click **Explore**, right-click **Local Disk (C:)**, and then click **Properties**. The file system in use—NTFS—is listed in the General tab, on the second line.

3. Create another account with limited rights. (This is done through the Control Panel.) Name the account **Limited Rights**.

4. Click **Start**, **Log Off**, click **Switch User**, and then click **Limited Rights**.

5. Open Windows Explorer. Navigate to **C:\Documents and Settings\\***Account with Administrative Rights* (replacing *Account with Administrative Rights* with any user account that has administrative rights on this computer). Note that Windows XP displays a warning that access is denied.

6. Log off and then log on with the account that has administrative rights.

7. Open Windows Explorer. Navigate to **C:\Documents and Settings\Limited Rights**. Note that Windows XP allows the folders to be accessed.

8. Log off and then log on as **Limited Rights**.

9. Open Windows Explorer, if necessary, and navigate to **C:\Documents and Settings\Limited Rights**. Right-click **Limited Rights**, and then click **Sharing and Security**. Click to select the **Make this folder private** check box, and then click **OK**. Click **No** to the resulting warning about passwords.

10. Log off and then log on with the account that has administrative rights. Open Windows Explorer, if necessary, and then navigate to **C:\Documents and Settings\Limited Rights**. Note that access is no longer permitted, as shown in Figure 11-1.

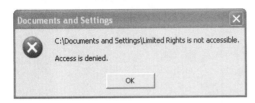

**Figure 11-1**   Access denied

11. Log off and then log on as **Limited Rights**. Open Windows Explorer, if necessary, and navigate to **C:\Documents and Settings\Limited Rights**. Right-click **Limited Rights**, and then click **Sharing and Security**. Click to clear the **Make this folder private** check box, and then click **OK**.

12. Open Notepad, type your name in the window, and then save the file as **Limited Rights File** in **C:\Documents and Settings\Limited Rights\**. Close Notepad.

13. In Windows Explorer, navigate to **Limited Rights File**, right-click the file, and then click **Properties**. Click the **Advanced** button to open the Advanced Attributes dialog box, shown in Figure 11-2, and then click to select the **Encrypt contents to secure data** check box. Notice that the Details button remains dimmed. Click **OK**, and then click **Apply**.

14. In the Encryption Warning dialog box (see Figure 11-3), click the **Encrypt the file only** option button, and then click **OK** twice. Notice that file listing details in the right pane have changed colors.

15. Open and close the file via Windows Explorer. It opens and closes as expected.

16. Log off and then log on with the account that has administrative rights. Open Windows Explorer, if necessary, and then navigate to **C:\Documents and Settings\Limited Rights**. When you try to open Limited Rights File, access is denied.

**11**

**Figure 11-2**     Preparing to encrypt content

**Figure 11-3**     Encrypting the file

17. Log off and then log on as **Limited Rights**. Open Windows Explorer, if necessary, and navigate to **C:\Documents and Settings\Limited Rights**.
Open and close Limited Rights File. Right-click **Limited Rights File**, click
**Properties**, click **Advanced**, and then click **Details**. Read the information in
the resulting dialog box, click the **Limited Rights** user name, click **Remove**,
and then click **OK**. Note that you are not allowed to remove all users from
this file. Click **OK**, and then click **Cancel**. Click to clear the **Encrypt contents to secure data** check box, and then click **OK**.

18. Click **OK** again, and then log off.

## Certification Objectives

Objectives for Microsoft Exam #70-272: Supporting Users and Troubleshooting Desktop
Applications on a Microsoft Windows XP Operating System:

➤ Troubleshoot insufficient user permissions and rights.

## Review Questions

1. One workstation can contain more than one My Pictures folder on its C: drive. True or False?

2. By default, remote access is disabled in Windows XP. True or False?

3. The "Encryption Details for:" dialog box lists the user name and the _____ name.

4. What are the two option buttons in the Encryption Warning dialog box?

5. By default, what two check boxes are selected in the Advanced Attributes dialog box?

---

# LAB 11.2 WORKING WITH LOST INFORMATION OR FILES

## Objectives

The goal of this lab is to acquaint you with a few ways in which end users can "lose" information on their workstations. In most situations, the information or file is not lost; it's merely not visible because of the selection of one option or another.

**11**

## Materials Required

This lab requires the following:

➤ A computer that runs Microsoft Windows XP and that is capable of booting to another operating system

➤ Office 2003

➤ Two accounts with administrative rights on the computer

➤ One account with limited rights on the computer

Estimated completion time: 15 minutes

## Activity Background

In this lab, you discover how a screen that appears to be "empty" of information can still provide access to that information; it's just a matter of knowing a few minor tricks.

**LAB ACTIVITY**

## ACTIVITY

1. Log on to the computer. You need to log on with administrative rights.

2. Click **Start**, point to **All Programs**, point to **Microsoft Office**, and then click **Microsoft Office Excel 2003**. (Allow Windows XP to install the application, if necessary.) Close the Task Pane, if necessary.

3. Type your name in cells A1 to A3. Type your name in the same range of cells for columns B and C, as shown in Figure 11-4.

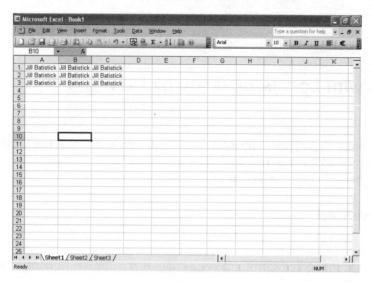

**Figure 11-4**    Preparing a range of cells

4. Click and hold on the Column **A** header, and then drag to highlight columns A, B, and C, as shown in Figure 11-5.

5. Right-click the highlighted area, and then click **Hide**. The columns disappear, and the first column shown is Column D. Click the first cell of Column D and notice that the Name Box above the column letter now shows D1. Right-click the Column **D** header, and then click **Unhide**. Your hidden columns do not reappear.

6. Click the **Name Box**, type **A1**, and then press **Enter**. Click **Format**, point to **Column**, and then click **Unhide**. Column A reappears.

7. Repeat Step 6 for columns B and C.

8. Save the file as **Lab 11.2 Spreadsheet** in **C:\Documents and Settings\***Your User Name***.

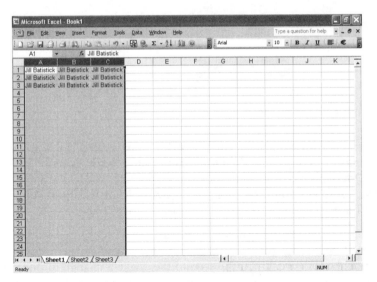

**Figure 11-5**   Highlighting a range of cells

9. Open Windows Explorer and navigate to the file you just created. Right-click the file, and then click **Properties**. Click the **General** tab, if necessary, and then click the **Hidden** check box. Click **OK**.

10. Log off and then log on with the second account that has administrative rights.

11. Open Windows Explorer and navigate to the location of the file you created in Step 8. You cannot see the spreadsheet. Click **Tools**, **Folder Options** from the menu, click the **View** tab, and then click the **Show hidden files and folders** option button. Click **OK**. The spreadsheet is displayed.

12. Click **Tools**, **Folder Options**, click the **View** tab, and then click the **Do not show hidden files and folders** option button. Click **OK**.

13. Log off and then log on with the account that has only limited rights.

14. Repeat Step 11 from within this account. Access is denied. The account doesn't even have the chance to try to use the Show hidden files and folders option button. Click **OK**.

15. Log off and then log on with the first account that has administrative rights. Open Windows Explorer and move the **Lab 11.2 Spreadsheet** file to **C:\Documents and Settings\All Users\Documents**. Copy and paste the file into the same location, using the default name Windows XP gives to the file, as shown in Figure 11-6.

16. Right-click the second file, click **Properties**, click the **General** tab, if necessary, and then click to select the **Read-only** check box. Click **OK**.

**Figure 11-6**   Creating a duplicate file

17. Log off and log on with the account that has only limited rights. Open Windows Explorer. Navigate to **C:\Documents and Settings\All Users\Documents**. You cannot see the files. Click **Tools, Folder Options**, click the **View** tab, and then click the **Show hidden files and folders** option button. Click **OK**. The files appear.

18. Open the first file (letting Windows XP walk you through the install process for Excel, if necessary), make a change to one cell, and then try to save the file. You can make the save. Open the second file, make a change to one cell, and then try to save the file. Click **OK** to the resulting warning box, shown in Figure 11-7, click **Cancel**, and then close Excel without saving the file.

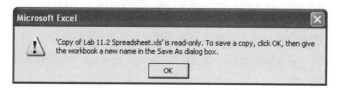

**Figure 11-7**   File saving is denied

19. Log off.

## Certification Objectives

Objectives for Microsoft Exam #70-272: Supporting Users and Troubleshooting Desktop Applications on a Microsoft Windows XP Operating System:

➤ Configure and troubleshoot application access on a multiple user client computer.

➤ Troubleshoot insufficient user permissions and rights.

## Review Questions

1. A file can have the read-only and hidden attributes activated at the same time. True or False?

2. The Summary tab of the Properties dialog box can have blank information boxes, but the Author information box is always filled in. True or False?

3. In Excel, you can move the focus of the spreadsheet to a cell that's not visible by typing the cell's column letter and row number into the

_____ .

4. A user with limited rights can't open a read-only file. True or False?

5. Files in C:\Documents and Settings\All Users\Documents can't be viewed by an account that has only limited rights. True or False?

---

# LAB 11.3 WORKING WITH QUOTAS

## Objectives

The goal of this lab is to explore the basic use of quotas in Windows XP. As technology progresses, hard drives are becoming bigger. Unfortunately, however, users are working with and saving more files and filling up those hard drives as fast as they are made. Keeping users as a group from overrunning your network's or workstation's storage capacity is important to your career as a DST.

**11**

## Materials Required

This lab requires the following:

➤ A computer that runs Microsoft Windows XP and that is capable of booting to another operating system

➤ Administrative rights on the computer

➤ The Limited Rights account from Lab 11.1

Estimated completion time: 15 minutes

## Activity Background

In this lab, you discover how easy it is to limit end users' storage usage. The threshold for the storage quota is set to a very low level for brevity in this lab, but it gives you a good idea of how easy it would be to rein in that one rogue end user who saves endless iterations of spreadsheets, word processing files, and Photoshop experimentations.

**LAB ACTIVITY**

## ACTIVITY

1. Log on to the computer. You need to log on with administrative rights.

2. Open Windows Explorer, right-click **Local Disk (C:)**, click **Properties**, and then click the **Quota** tab. Notice that disk quotas are disabled by default.

3. Click to select the **Enable quota management** check box and the **Deny disk space to users exceeding quota limit** check box.

4. Click the **Limit disk space to** option button, set the limit level to **10 KB**, and then set the warning level to **5 KB**. Click the **Quota Entries** button. Your screen should resemble Figure 11-8.

 **NOTE** Your screen can differ greatly. It depends on how many times this lab has been done. It also depends on how many lab users have failed to clear their activities before they went to their next class.

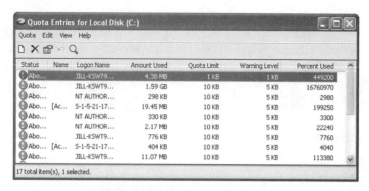

**Figure 11-8**   Quota information

5. Click **Quota, New Quota Entry** from the menu. Type **Limited Rights** in the text box, and then click **OK**. Click the **Limit disk space to** option button, if necessary, enter **10 KB** in the first text box set, and then enter **5 KB** in the second text box set. Click **OK**. Close the dialog box.

6. Click **OK** in the Properties dialog box. When the message box shown in Figure 11-9 is displayed, click **OK**. Wait while Windows XP performs the scan.

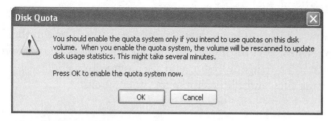

**Figure 11-9**   Warning of an impending scan

7. Log off and log on as **Limited Rights**. Open Microsoft Word.

8. Type your name in the document, click **Insert** on the menu bar, point to **Picture**, and click **From File**. Double-click **Sample Pictures**, select multiple pictures in the dialog box (*Hint:* Hold down the Ctrl button as you click each one), and then click **Insert**. Press **Ctrl+S**, accept the default name, and then click the **Save** button. Read the resulting warning message. Click **OK**, and then click **Cancel**. Close Word without saving the changes.

9. Log off as Limited Rights and log on with your full administrative account. Open Windows Explorer, right-click **Local Disk (C:)**, click **Properties**, and then click the **Quota** tab. Click to clear the **Enable quota management** check box, and then click **OK**. Click **OK** to the warning box.

10. Log off and log on as **Limited Rights**. Open Microsoft Word and try to repeat the action in Step 8. This time your file saving isn't restricted.

11. Close Microsoft Word, and log off.

## Certification Objectives

Objectives for Microsoft Exam #70-272: Supporting Users and Troubleshooting Desktop Applications on a Microsoft Windows XP Operating System:

➤ Troubleshoot insufficient user permissions and rights.

## Review Questions

1. In Windows XP, disk quotas are _____ by default.

2. You can enable quota management in Windows XP without limited disk usage. True or False?

3. The default warning level for exceeding disk usage is _____ .

4. A disk quota can affect an account with administrative rights, even if that account is the only account on the system with administrative rights. True or False?

5. When you enable disk quotas on your system, what is the purpose of the resulting scan that Windows XP performs?

## LAB **11.4** WORKING WITH PERMISSIONS

### Objectives

The goal of this lab is to explore the intricacies of permissions on a Windows XP workstation. (Permission is defined as what the end user can do with an object, such as a file or folder.) By using permissions—which include Full Control, Modify, Read & Execute, List Folder Contents, Read, Write, and Special Permissions—you can fine-tune what you permit to be done to your object (in this case, a file or folder).

## Materials Required

This lab requires the following:

➤  A computer that runs Microsoft Windows XP and is capable of booting to another operating system

➤  Administrative rights on the computer

➤  Completion of Lab 11.1

Estimated completion time: 15 minutes

## Activity Background

In this lab, you discover that changing just one permission changes an end user's entire work experience. Note that although your organization would most likely grant and deny permissions based on group membership, exploring permissions as shown in the lab can still give you a feel for how they affect an end user's access to a resource.

**ACTIVITY**

1. Log on to the computer as **Limited Rights**. Open Windows Explorer, and try to open **C:\Documents and Settings\*Your Administrator Account*.** Access is denied. Log off from this account.

2. Log on to the computer. You need to log on with administrative rights.

3. Open Windows Explorer and navigate to **C:\Documents and Settings\*Your User Name*.** Right-click your user name folder, and then click **Properties**. Notice that you do not have a Security tab in this dialog box. Click **Cancel**.

4. Click **Start**, **Control Panel**. If necessary, click **Switch to Classic View**. Double-click **Folder Options**. Click the **View** tab, scroll the list box to the end of the list, and then click to clear the **Use simple file sharing (Recommended)** check box, as shown in Figure 11-10. Click **OK**.

5. In Windows Explorer, right-click your user name folder, and then click **Properties**. Notice that you now have a Security tab in this dialog box. Click the **Security** tab.

6. Click **Add**. Type **Limited Rights** in the text box, and then click **OK**. Notice the change in the list of permissions at the bottom of the Security tab. Click **OK**.

7. Open Notepad, type your name and the date in the file, and save it as **Permissions Test** to **C:\Documents and Settings\*Your User Name*.** Close Notepad.

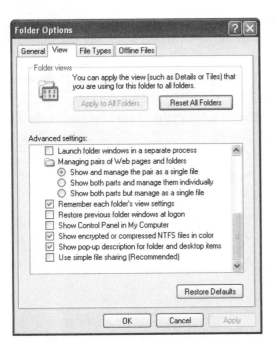

**Figure 11-10**  Removing simple file sharing

8. Log off and log on as **Limited Rights**. Open Windows Explorer, and try to open **C:\Documents and Settings\\*Your Administrator Account***. Access is now permitted. Double-click the **Permissions Test** file. The file opens. Type **First Test** at the end of the document, click **File**, and then click **Save**. Read the warning dialog box stating that you cannot create this file. Click **OK**, click **Cancel**, and then close Notepad without trying to save the changes.

9. In Windows Explorer, try to delete the file. Access is denied. Click **OK**.

10. Log off and then log back on with the account that has full administrative privileges.

11. Open Windows Explorer and navigate to **C:\Documents and Settings\\*Your User Name***. Right-click your user name folder, click **Properties**, and click the **Security** tab. Click the **Limited Rights** entry at the top of the Security tab, and then click the **Modify** check box under the Allow column at the bottom of the tab. Click the **Advanced** button to view the information about this account and others. Click **OK**, and then click **OK** again.

12. Log off and log on as **Limited Rights**. Open Windows Explorer, and try to open **C:\Documents and Settings\\*Your Administrator Account***. Double-click the **Permissions Test** file. The file opens. Type **Second Test** at the end of the document, click **File**, and then click **Save**. Windows XP allows you to save a new version of the file that overwrites the old version. (You can check

the time stamp in Windows Explorer to confirm.) Click **File**, **Save As** from the menu. Type **Permissions Test Number Two** as the file name and then click **Save**. Close Notepad.

13. In Windows Explorer, try to delete **Permissions Test** and **Permissions Test Number Two**. You can successfully delete both.

14. As time permits, explore other combinations of permissions for the Limited Rights account.

15. Log off.

## Certification Objectives

Objectives for Microsoft Exam #70-272: Supporting Users and Troubleshooting Desktop Applications on a Microsoft Windows XP Operating System:

➤ Configure and troubleshoot file system access and file permission problems on multiboot computers.

## Review Questions

1. You can set permissions on a computer that is not connected to a domain. True or False?

2. If simple file sharing is not in use on an Administrator account that's not connected to a domain, what tabs show up in the respective Properties dialog box?

3. What are the default permissions listed in the Security tab of the Properties dialog box, when the tab is available?

4. If the Security tab of the Properties dialog box is open to list the default permissions of a limited account and if you select the Modify check box, what other check box is selected by default?

5. What are the four tabs in the Advanced Security Settings dialog box?

# CONFIGURE APPLICATION SECURITY

## Labs included in this chapter:

➤ Lab 12.1 Exploring Virus Protection Software

➤ Lab 12.2 Working with Macros

➤ Lab 12.3 Working with Password Restrictions

➤ Lab 12.4 Working with a Password Reset Disk

| Microsoft MCDST Exam #70-272 Objectives | |
|---|---|
| Objective | Lab |
| Troubleshoot access to local resources. | 12.3, 12.4 |
| Troubleshoot insufficient user permissions and rights. | 12.3, 12.4 |
| Answer end-user questions related to security incidents. | 12.2 |
| Identify a virus attack. | 12.1 |

# LAB 12.1 EXPLORING VIRUS PROTECTION SOFTWARE

## Objectives

The goal of this lab is to become familiar with some features available in Norton AntiVirus software. Although the features in this software aren't identical to other software products—such as McAfee VirusScan—exploring the options makes you more skilled at virus protection at the micro level, which is at the workstation or freestanding computer. Virus protection at the macro level—that is, at the network level—is dictated by the IT teams in your organization and is beyond the scope of this lab.

## Materials Required

This lab requires the following:

➤ A computer that runs Microsoft Windows XP

➤ An account with administrative rights on the computer

➤ Norton AntiVirus installed on the workstation or computer

➤ Internet access

Estimated completion time: 15 minutes

## Activity Background

In this lab, you learn about some informational features of Norton AntiVirus. Becoming proficient in finding and interpreting this information is vital to your career as a DST.

### ACTIVITY

1. Log on to the computer. You need to log on with administrative rights.

2. Mouse over the **Norton AntiVirus** icon in the notification area. Note that it's auto-protect enabled.

You can start the program from the notification area, if necessary, but you should also know about the other method, shown in Step 3.

3. Click **Start**, point to **All Programs**, point to **Norton Internet Security**, point to **Norton AntiVirus**, and then click **Norton AntiVirus**. Your screen should resemble Figure 12-1. Note that the check marks change depending on system status—be sure to read the information on the right side of the screen.

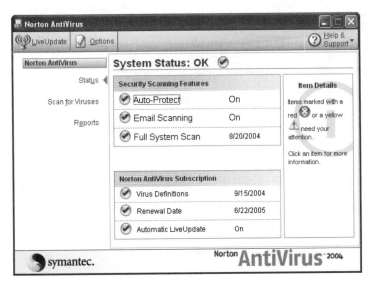

**Figure 12-1**    The Norton AntiVirus window

4. Read the information in the Item Details pane on the right, and then click **Reports** on the left side. Your screen should resemble Figure 12-2.

**12**

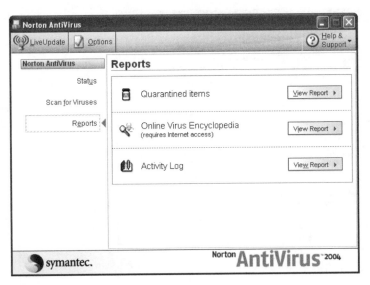

**Figure 12-2**    The Reports window

5. Click the **View Report** button in the Quarantined items section. Performing this step on the author's computer produced Figure 12-3. Notice the list of threats. The items listed on your computer will vary depending on your computer's use on the Internet or intranet.

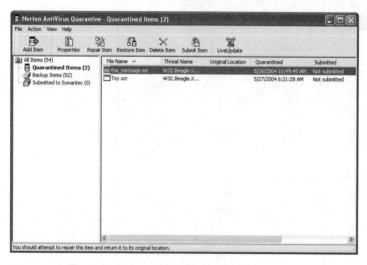

**Figure 12-3**   List of threats

6. Click the **Backup Items** link on the left side. Performing this step on the author's computer produced Figure 12-4. Notice the list of threats. Your list will differ. Close the window.

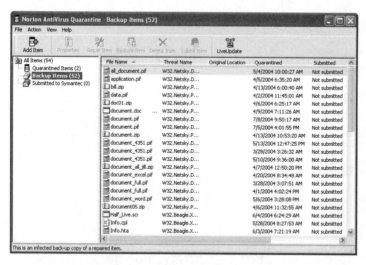

**Figure 12-4**   Copies of files that were infected

7. Connect to the Internet, and then click the **View Report** button in the Online Virus Encyclopedia section (shown previously in Figure 12-2). This step takes you to the Symantec Web site. (Symantec produces the Norton line of software.)

8. Click the **W** link. Scroll down to and click the **W32.Beagle.X@mm** link. Read the information about this worm, click the **Back** button, scroll down to and click the **SW32.Netsky.D@mm** link, and read the information about this worm.

9. Go to **www.google.com** and perform similar searches on these two worms.

10. Close Internet Explorer and disconnect from the Internet.

11. Log off.

## Certification Objectives

Objectives for Microsoft Exam #70-272: Supporting Users and Troubleshooting Desktop Applications on a Microsoft Windows XP Operating System:

➤ Identify a virus attack.

### REVIEW QUESTIONS

1. When Norton AntiVirus is correctly installed, it places a related icon in the Notification Area of your desktop. True or False?

2. By default, Norton AntiVirus is auto-enabled on a workstation. True or False?

3. What are the three categories of items in the Quarantined Items window in Norton AntiVirus?

4. You can view the Online Virus Encyclopedia offline. True or False?

5. In the Norton AntiVirus window, describe the icon that indicates items are up-to-date.

**12**

## LAB 12.2 WORKING WITH MACROS

### Objectives

The goal of this lab is to take a low-level look at macros. Macros were originally conceived to help end users and administrators alike with repetitive tasks. Unfortunately, they now can be used maliciously to damage end user files and applications, and they can travel to workstations via e-mail attachments. If your end user opens an attachment that runs an unwanted macro, the results can be disastrous.

### Materials Required

This lab requires the following:

➤ A computer that runs Microsoft Windows XP

➤ An account with administrative rights on the computer

➤    An account with limited rights on the computer

| Estimated completion time: 15 minutes |
| --- |

## Activity Background

In this lab, you build and run a simple macro. Even with this limited lab, you can see the damage a macro can inflict—in the blink of an eye.

**LAB ACTIVITY**

### ACTIVITY

1. Log on to the computer. You need to log on with administrative rights.

2. Click **Start**, point to **All Programs**, point to **Microsoft Office**, and then click **Microsoft Office Word 2003**. Close the Task Pane, if necessary.

3. Click **Tools** on the menu bar, point to **Macro**, and then click **Macros**. Your screen should resemble Figure 12-5.

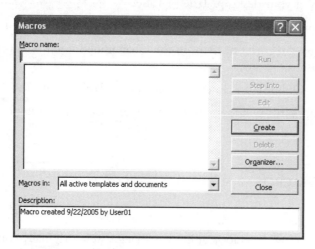

**Figure 12-5**    Starting to build a macro

4. Type **TestMacro** in the Macro name text box, and then click **Create**. Your screen should resemble Figure 12-6. This is the window where you could build the code behind the macro by hand, should you choose to do so. Press **Alt+F11** to return to Word.

5. Click **Tools** on the menu bar, point to **Macro**, and then click **Record New Macro**. Type **TestTwoMacro** in the Macro name text box, click the **Keyboard** button, press **Alt+T** to enter this key combination into the Press

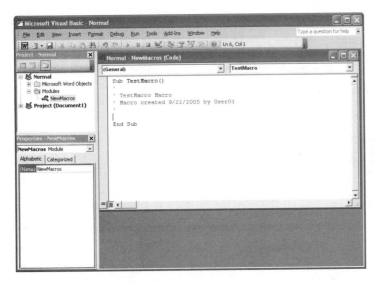

**Figure 12-6**   Code screen

new shortcut key text box, and then click **Assign**. Click **Close**. Notice the floating Macro toolbar and the changed pointer on the screen, as shown in Figure 12-7.

**Figure 12-7**   Recording a macro

6. Press **Ctrl+A**, press the **Delete** key, type **I've erased all your work.**, and then click the **Stop Recording** button on the Macro toolbar.

7. Press **Alt+Tab** to return to the Visual Basic screen. Note the code that you, fortunately, didn't have to type by hand. Press **Alt+Tab** to return to Word.

8. Press **Ctrl+N** to open a new document, and then type **This is the most important document of my life**. Press **Alt+F8**. Click **TestTwoMacro**, and then click **Run**. The content on your screen changes. Scary, isn't it?

9. If your instructor requires it, remove the macro from the Macros dialog box.

10. If time permits, try to repeat this lab with the limited rights account.

11. Close Word without saving changes to your documents, close any other open windows, and log off.

## Certification Objectives

Objectives for Microsoft Exam #70-272: Supporting Users and Troubleshooting Desktop Applications on a Microsoft Windows XP Operating System:

➤ Answer end-user questions related to security incidents.

LAB ACTIVITY

### REVIEW QUESTIONS

1. Shortcut keys can be assigned only by Windows XP. True or False?
2. In the Customize Keyboard dialog box, commands are saved by default to the _____ template.
3. In Word, you can open the Macros dialog box by pressing _____ .
4. What macro information is included by default in the Description text box in the Macros dialog box?
5. You must have administrative privileges to build a macro in an Office application. True or False?

## LAB 12.3 WORKING WITH PASSWORD RESTRICTIONS

### Objectives

The goal of this lab is to become acquainted with what end users see when they bump up against password restrictions on their workstations. Most users are comfortable with entering user name and password combinations; however, when they encounter problems associated with setting passwords, they might not understand the restrictions, especially if the restrictions have been implemented *after* they last set their passwords.

### Materials Required

This lab requires the following:

➤ A computer that runs Microsoft Windows XP

➤ An account with administrative rights on the computer

➤ An account that has limited rights on the computer and that has no password protection

Estimated completion time: 15 minutes

## Activity Background

In this lab, you find yourself in the end user's seat—which is a good place to visit if you're fielding DST calls from end users who are all chiming the same thing: "But it used to work this way before!"

**LAB ACTIVITY**

## ACTIVITY

1. Log on to the computer that does not have administrative rights. Note that you're not prompted for a password.

2. Log off and log on with the account that has administrative privileges.

3. Click **Start**, **Control Panel**. If necessary, click **Switch to Classic View**. Double-click **Administrative Tools**, and then double-click **Local Security Policy**. Your screen should resemble Figure 12-8.

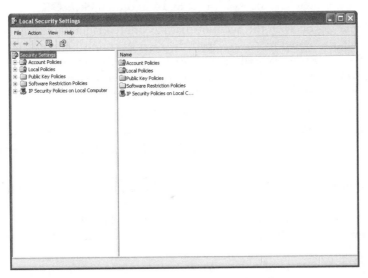

**Figure 12-8**   The Local Security Settings window

4. Double-click **Account Policies** in the left pane, and then double-click **Password Policy**. Right-click **Enforce password history**, and then click **Properties**. Type **1** in the passwords remembered list box, and then click **OK**. Examine the possible password settings, and notice the change in the Security Setting value for Enforce password history.

5. Log off and log on with the account that has limited rights. Click **Start**, **Control Panel**, and then double-click **User Accounts**. Click **Create a password**, type **Password1** in both password text boxes, and then click **Create Password**. Close the User Accounts window, and close Control Panel.

6. Log off the limited user account and then log back on, entering the new password when prompted to do so. Click **Start**, **Control Panel**, and then double-click **User Accounts**. Click **Change my password**, type **Password1** in all three password text boxes, and then click **Change Password**. You see a User Accounts warning message stating that the password does not meet password policy requirements. (In this case, you reused the previous password, which is not permitted per the settings made in Step 4.) Click **OK**.

7. Type **Password2** in the second and third password text boxes, and then click **Change Password**.

8. Close all open windows, and log off.

9. Log on with the account that has administrative privileges. Return to the Local Security Settings window. Click to expand **Account Policies** and then **Password Policy**. Right-click **Minimum password length**, and then click **Properties**. Set the characters list box to **10**, and then click **OK**.

10. Log off and log on with the account that has limited rights, entering the password when prompted to do so. Open the User Accounts window, and then click **Change my password**. Type **Password2** in the first text box, and type **Password3** in the second and third text boxes. Click **Change Password**. You receive the same warning as in Step 6, but this time it's for a different reason—the password is too short. Click **OK**.

11. Type **Password03** in the second and third text boxes, type **It rhymes with tree.** in the fourth text box, and then click **Change Password**. The password change is accepted.

12. Close all open windows, and log off. Click the same user account name, and type **Password1** as the password. Press **Enter**. The pop-up message balloon tells you that you can click the blue question mark button for help on entering passwords. Click the question mark button to see your password hint.

**NOTE**

This button is particularly helpful when your end user, frustrated and in a hurry, says, "I don't remember my password and I certainly don't remember my hint!"

13. Type **Password03** in the text box and then press **Enter**. You successfully log on. Log off and log on with the account that has administrative privileges. Open User Accounts (via Control Panel), double-click the account you used in Step 12, and click **Change the password**. Your screen should resemble Figure 12-9. Notice the effect your password change would have on this account, and note that you wouldn't need the user's current password to make the change. Click **Cancel**, and close the User Accounts window.

This password change feature of User Accounts can be useful if you need to do a quick lockout on an account.

**TIP**

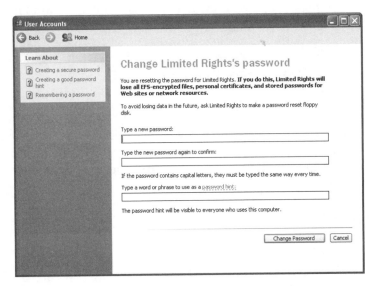

**Figure 12-9**   Changing the password of a limited account

14. Log off.

## Certification Objectives

Objectives for Microsoft Exam #70-272: Supporting Users and Troubleshooting Desktop Applications on a Microsoft Windows XP Operating System:

➤ Troubleshoot access to local resources.

➤ Troubleshoot insufficient user permissions and rights.

### REVIEW QUESTIONS

1. In the Local Security Settings window, under Password Policy, you can set the Minimum password length and the Minimum password _____ .

2. In the Local Security Settings window, the Enforce password history value is set to _____ by default.

3. In the Local Security Settings window, under Password Policy, what two policies are set to disabled by default?

12

4. End users with limited rights on their accounts can change their own passwords and also have passwords changed without their permission. True or
   False?

5. In the logon screen in Windows XP, the blue question mark icon appears after
   an unsuccessful logon only when the respective account is password protected.
   True or False?

---

# LAB 12.4 WORKING WITH A PASSWORD RESET DISK

## Objectives

The goal of this lab is to learn how to create a password reset disk. Having a password reset
disk around is as potentially dangerous as allowing your end users to write their passwords
on sticky notes stuck to their monitors. If you allow users to create these disks, make sure the
disks are stored in a secure location.

## Materials Required

This lab requires the following:

➤ A computer that runs Microsoft Windows XP

➤ An account with administrative rights on the computer

➤ A floppy disk and a floppy disk drive on the computer

Estimated completion time: 15 minutes

## Activity Background

In this lab, you learn that a password reset disk creates a vulnerability on a workstation; to
counteract that vulnerability, you configure a screen saver to lock the workstation when it's
not in use. That way, unauthorized personnel can't come to an unattended workstation and
make a password reset disk for later use.

LAB ACTIVITY

## ACTIVITY

1. Log on to the computer. You need to log on with administrative rights.

2. Through the User Accounts window, create a new user with administrative
   rights. Name the user **PasswordDisk**. Set the password to **PasswordDisk**.

3. Log off and log on as **PasswordDisk**, supplying the password when prompted
   to do so.

4. Click **Start**, **Control Panel**, and double-click **User Accounts**. Click **PasswordDisk**, and then on the left side of the screen, click **Prevent a forgotten password**. The Forgotten Password Wizard starts, shown in Figure 12-10.

**Figure 12-10**   The Forgotten Password Wizard

5. Click **Next**, insert the blank formatted disk, and then click **Next**.

6. Click **Next**, read the warning, click **OK**, type **PasswordDisk**, and then click **Next**. Wait while Windows XP creates the password reset disk, as shown in Figure 12-11. Click **Next**. Click **Finish**. Remove the disk from the drive.

7. Close all open windows, and log off the PasswordDisk account.

8. Click the **PasswordDisk** account in the logon window, and then type **Password**. Press **Enter**. Notice the balloon message stating that you can use your password reset disk to log on. Click the link; the wizard opens.

9. Click **Next**, insert the disk into the drive, and then click **Next**. Type **PasswordDisk2** in the first and second text boxes, and then click **Next**. Click **Finish**.

10. In the logon window, type **PasswordDisk2**, and then press **Enter**. You have logged on successfully.

11. Open Microsoft Word, type your name, click **Tools**, and then click **Options** to open the Options dialog box.

12. Press the **Windows key+D**, right-click the desktop, and then click **Properties**. Click the **Screen Saver** tab, change the Wait list box to **1**, and then click **OK**. Wait until the screen saver appears, and then move your

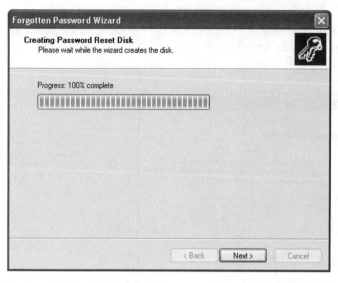

**Figure 12-11**    Windows XP creates the password reset disk

mouse. Click the **PasswordDisk** logon name, type **PasswordDisk2**, and then press **Enter**. You are returned to where you left off in Word, at the Options dialog box.

**NOTE**

As you can see, setting a screen saver in this manner effectively locks the workstation when the end user steps away without logging off.

13. As time permits, work through the wizard for other accounts.

14. Close all open windows, and log off.

## Certification Objectives

Objectives for Microsoft Exam #70-272: Supporting Users and Troubleshooting Desktop Applications on a Microsoft Windows XP Operating System:

➤ Troubleshoot access to local resources.

➤ Troubleshoot insufficient user permissions and rights.

**LAB ACTIVITY**

## REVIEW QUESTIONS

1. You open the Forgotten Password Wizard through the _____ window.

2. After you have created a password reset disk, you can use it only once to reset a password. After that, you must create a new password reset disk. True or False?

3. Your account need not be password protected for you to build a password reset disk. True or False?

4. One floppy disk can hold password reset information for multiple user accounts. True or False?

5. You must have a failed logon before you have a chance to use a password reset disk. True or False?

**12**

# MANAGE OFFICE APPLICATION UPDATES AND UPGRADES

---

## Labs included in this chapter:

➤ Lab 13.1 Working with Windows Updates

➤ Lab 13.2 Understanding Add-Ins

➤ Lab 13.3 Hunting Information in a Microsoft Newsgroup

---

| Microsoft MCDST Exam #70-272 Objectives | |
|---|---|
| Objective | Lab |
| Applying critical updates. | 13.1 |

# LAB 13.1 WORKING WITH WINDOWS UPDATES

## Objectives

The goal of this lab is to become familiar with updating Windows XP. Of course, in a large corporate network that employs multiple DSTs, you won't be in charge of acquiring, testing, or deploying Windows updates. However, being familiar with the update process on a lone workstation gives you a feel for the process so that you can help end users and other IT professionals in your organization when such updates are pushed across your network.

## Materials Required

This lab requires the following:

➤ A computer that runs Microsoft Windows XP

➤ An account with administrative rights on the computer

➤ Windows XP updates that have been downloaded but not yet installed

➤ Automatic Updates set to "Download updates for me, but let me choose when to install them" (through Control Panel, System, Automatic Updates or Control Panel, Performance and Maintenance, System, Automatic Updates)

➤ One other installation of third-party software (optional)

Estimated completion time: 15 minutes

## Activity Background

In this lab, you watch the process of Windows updating and get a feel for how the notification area works.

LAB ACTIVITY

## ACTIVITY

1. Log on to the computer. You need to log on with administrative rights.

2. Observe the notification area on your desktop, as shown in Figure 13-1. Your notification area might differ, depending on the software loaded on your workstation.

**Figure 13-1**   Notification area

3. Click the **arrow** button on the left side of the notification area to expand the display of buttons, as shown in Figure 13-2. (Look for the icon that's a globe with the Microsoft flag flying over it; that's the Windows Update icon.)

**Figure 13-2**   Expanded display

4. Right-click a blank spot in the notification area. Your screen should resemble Figure 13-3.

**Figure 13-3**   The shortcut menu for the notification area

5. Click **Properties**. Your screen should resemble Figure 13-4.

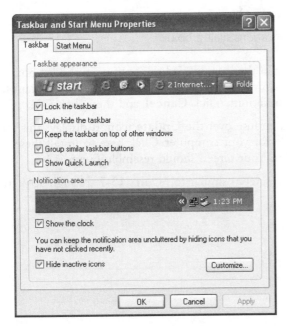

**Figure 13-4**   The Taskbar tab

6. Click to clear the **Hide inactive icons** check box, and click **Apply**. Note that the arrow is no longer on the left side of the notification area. Click the

**13**

check box again, and then click **Apply**. The arrow in the notification area returns. Click the **Customize** button. Your screen should resemble Figure 13-5.

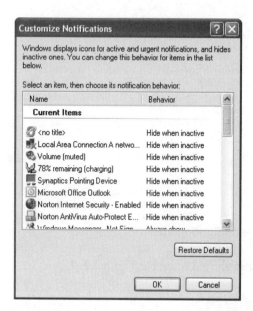

**Figure 13-5**    The Customize Notifications dialog box

7. Click the first Behavior in the list and read the options in the list box. As you can see, it is in this window that you can select which icons you want to display and under what conditions. Click **Cancel**, and then click **OK**.

8. In the notification area, mouse over the **Update** icon. It displays this information: "Updates are ready for your computer. Click here to install these updates." Click the icon. Your screen should resemble Figure 13-6.

9. Click **Install**. You'll see screens similar to Figures 13-7 through 13-9 as the installation progresses.

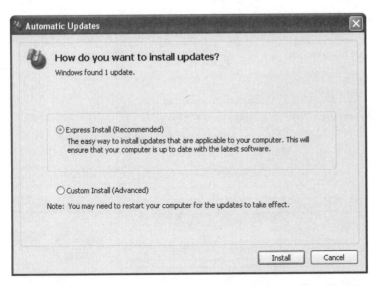

**Figure 13-6**   The Automatic Updates window

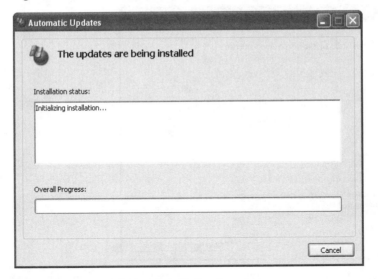

**Figure 13-7**   Installation is initialized

13

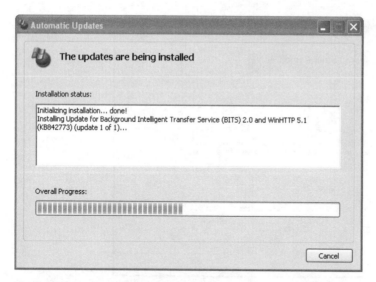

**Figure 13-8** Installation in progress

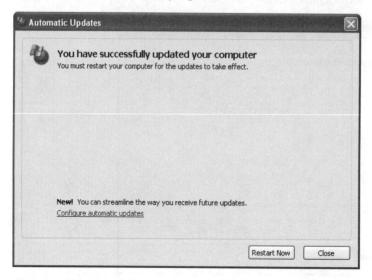

**Figure 13-9** Computer has been updated

 Of course, your screens will differ depending on the updates you're installing.

**NOTE**

10. Click **Configure automatic updates**. Your screen should resemble Figure 13-10.

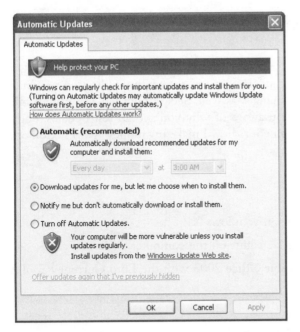

**Figure 13-10**   The Automatic Updates dialog box

13

11.  As time permits, explore the options and links on this page.

12.  Close all open windows, and log off.

## Certification Objectives

Objectives for Microsoft Exam #70-272: Supporting Users and Troubleshooting Desktop Applications on a Microsoft Windows XP Operating System:

➤  Applying critical updates.

## Review Questions

1.  When you use Automatic Updates in Windows XP, what two installation options do you have?

2.  If you choose to automatically download and install updates in Windows XP, you can set the day and time for that action to occur. True or False?

3.  In the Automatic Updates dialog box, the Automatic option is the recommended option. True or False?

4.  You must be connected to the Internet for manually downloaded updates to be installed. True or False?

5.  Windows XP always forces a restart of your computer after installing updates. True or False?

## LAB 13.2 UNDERSTANDING ADD-INS

### Objectives

The goal of this lab is to learn that add-ins don't just affect the application to which they are added—the system information changes as well. Seeing how fast the system information picks up on this change makes you aware of why you should test updates, upgrades, and add-ins before they are deployed on your "how I make my money" workstation or network.

### Materials Required

This lab requires the following:

➤ A computer that runs Microsoft Windows XP

➤ An account with administrative rights on the computer

➤ A fresh installation of Microsoft Office 2003 with the Euro Currency Tool Add-in not installed

Estimated completion time: 15 minutes

### Activity Background

In this lab, you watch how the effect of an add-in ripples through a workstation's environment.

**LAB ACTIVITY**

### ACTIVITY

1. Log on to the computer. You need to log on with administrative rights.

2. Click **Start**, point to **All Programs**, point to **Microsoft Office**, and then click **Microsoft Office Excel 2003**. Close the Task Pane, if necessary.

3. Type **1000** in the first cell, and then press **Enter**. Right-click the cell, click **Format Cells**, and then click **Currency**. Click the **Symbol** list arrow, and scroll through the choices. Note that the symbol for the euro is not there. Click **Cancel**.

4. Press **Ctrl+S** and then save the file as **First File Name*XX-YY-ZZ*** (*XX-YY-ZZ* is the numerical representation of the month, day, and two-digit year). Accept the default location, and then click **Save**.

5. Click **Help, About Microsoft Office Excel** from the menu. Click the **Disabled Items** button. Your screen should resemble Figure 13-11. Note that no items are listed here. This should be no surprise. Your fresh installation has not given the software a chance to have anything go wrong. Click **Close**.

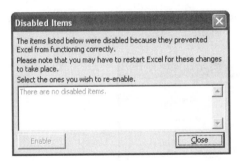

**Figure 13-11**   The Disabled Items dialog box

6. Click **System Info**. In the left pane, expand **Office 2003 applications**, and then expand **Microsoft Office Excel 2003**. Click **Active Workbook**. Your screen resembles Figure 13-12. Notice that the name of your file shows up at the top of the right pane.

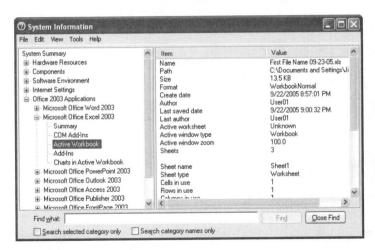

**Figure 13-12**   Viewing your file name

7. Press **Alt+Tab** to return to the Excel window. Click **File**, **Save As**. Name the file as **Second File NameXX-YY-ZZ** (*XX-YY-ZZ* is the numerical representation of the month, day, and two-digit year). Accept the default location, and then click **Save**. Press **Alt+Tab** to return to the System Information window. Note that the file name has not changed. Click **View**, **Refresh** from the menu, and see the file name change.

The Refresh command is your friend. If you make a change to your system and don't see it show up right away, don't panic—just use the Refresh command. You can always panic later.

**NOTE**

8. Click **Add-Ins**, and then scroll the right pane until it resembles Figure 13-13. Notice that eurotool.xla is not installed.

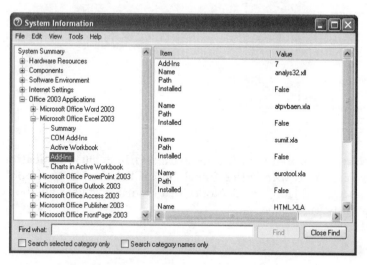

**Figure 13-13**    Viewing add-ins

9. Press **Alt+Tab**. Click **Tools**, **Add-Ins** from the menu. Click the **Euro Currency Tools** check box, as shown in Figure 13-14, and then click **OK**. Click **Yes** to the resulting message box, and wait while the component is installed.

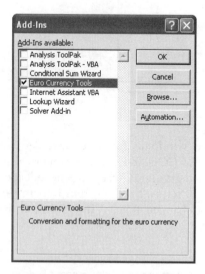

**Figure 13-14**    Available add-ins

10. The EuroValue toolbar appears on your screen. Right-click the toolbar and note that its name shows up on the resulting screen. Press **Esc**. Press **Alt+Tab** to reach the System Information window. Note that eurotool.xla still shows up as not installed.

11. Click **View**, **Refresh** from the menu. The eurotool.xla file now shows up as installed. Press **Alt+Tab**. Right-click the cell in which you typed 1000, and then click **Format Cells**. Click the **Number** tab, if necessary, and then click **Currency**. Click the **Symbol** list arrow, and scroll down until you find the Euro entries, as shown in Figure 13-15.

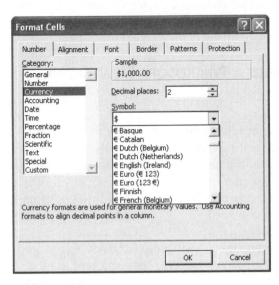

**Figure 13-15**  Euro entries

12. Select the first **Euro** entry, and then click **OK**. Notice the formatting change in cell A1. Experiment with the list box on the EuroValue toolbar as time permits.

13. Close all open windows. Do not save any changes.

14. Log off.

## Certification Objectives

Objectives for Microsoft Exam #70-272: Supporting Users and Troubleshooting Desktop Applications on a Microsoft Windows XP Operating System:

➤  None—Informational only

## Review Questions

1. The Disabled Items dialog box in an Office 2003 application always has items that you can re-enable. True or False?

2. What three buttons—besides OK—are available in the About Microsoft Excel window?

3. What is the default value in the list box on the EuroValue toolbar?

4. What is the file extension for an add-in in Excel?

5. The key combination Ctrl+R refreshes the screen in the System Information window. True or False?

---

# LAB 13.3 HUNTING INFORMATION IN A MICROSOFT NEWSGROUP

## Objectives

The goal of this lab is to become familiar with newsgroups at microsoft.com. These newsgroups might not be your first choice for information, but they can be helpful to keep as backup resources. Of course, most of the time, the information you need to support end users is available on your own workstation or your own network, so you won't often be driven out to newsgroups for answers to odd little questions. However, sometimes these freewheeling resources are just what you need.

**NOTE**

Of course, "freewheeling" often means "constantly changing." As you go through this lab, you'll no doubt find that links have come and gone and that names on the screen have changed. At times like these, it's best to keep moving; when a link no longer exists, use what you've learned so far in this lab manual to pick the obvious replacement link or on-screen element. After all, being a DST sometimes requires you to think beyond a rote sequence of clicks.

## Materials Required

This lab requires the following:

➤ A computer that runs Microsoft Windows XP

➤ An account with administrative rights on the computer

➤ Internet access

Estimated completion time: 15 minutes

## Activity Background

In this lab, you discover that Microsoft newsgroups are a great source of information. Of course, always protect your personal information while going online. Just because it's a friendly and easy environment in which to navigate doesn't mean you should let your guard down—it's still a public access area.

**LAB ACTIVITY**

### ACTIVITY

1. Log on to the computer. You need to log on with administrative rights.

2. Connect to the Internet and navigate to **http://www.support. microsoft.com/**. Click the **Search the Knowledge Base** link.

**NOTE**

Assume for the purposes of this lab that you're having trouble with PowerPoint locking up your computer.

3. Type **powerpoint locks up computer with cable modem** in the Search for text box, and then press **Enter**. Read the resulting links, and (with the exception of the PowerPoint Support Center link) click through a few of them and read the contents. Overall, the group of links doesn't look too promising, does it?

4. Click the **PowerPoint Support Center Link**. (*Note*: If that's not available, type **http://support.microsoft.com/default.aspx?scid=fh;EN-US;ppt** into your Address box.) Your screen should be similar to Figure 13-16.

**13**

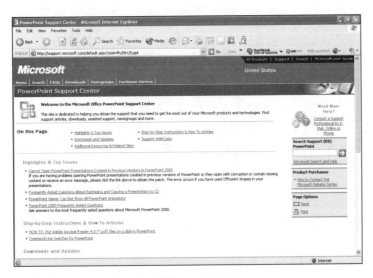

**Figure 13-16** PowerPoint Support Center

5. Type **powerpoint locks up computer with cable modem** in the Search Support (KB) PowerPoint box on the right, and then press **Enter**. Notice that you're looped back to what you saw in Step 3.

6. Navigate to **http://support.microsoft.com/newsgroups/default.aspx**. Your screen should be similar to Figure 13-17.

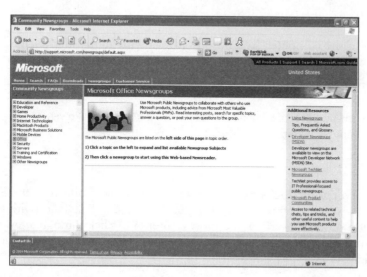

**Figure 13-17**   Microsoft Office newsgroups

7. Expand **Office**, if necessary, and then expand **PowerPoint**. Click the **PowerPoint** subheading, and then click the **Search** button in the middle of the window. Your screen should be similar to Figure 13-18.

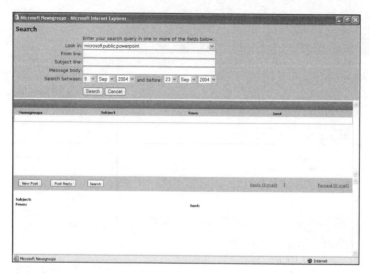

**Figure 13-18**   Starting a search